# Sober and Awake

a spiritual journey to hope, love
and the Power within

# Sober and Awake

a spiritual journey to hope, love
and the Power within

Patrick Webster

*Dedicated to the dozens of men and women
who have shown me a way to recover
and to those who have directed
me to a path of spiritual
discovery and
exploration*
♥

# Table of Contents

# Introduction

This book is a story of coming to sobriety first and then being awakened to a path. In my view and experience, to be spiritually awake is not to believe I have reached a final height of awareness, but to have reached an awareness of a path of incremental expansion of understanding; and then to realize I am left with no want greater than to expand that awareness.

I know there are people out there dealing with some or all of the same things I've dealt with, and continue to deal with: fear, self-loathing, self-defeatism, "wondering how I seem to repeatedly get in my own way", "wondering how in the world to deal with the curve-balls life seems to continually throw", addiction, alcoholism, and so many more.

I wanted to write a book that might shine a light on an opened door. On the other side of that door, we can see that the conditions of our lives, as we perceive them, don't have the power to define who we are. The circumstances in which we find ourselves do not have the final say on who we are.

*I came to this path* of discovery through the disease of alcoholism and addiction. But even people I know who have had no issue with addiction or dependence on alcohol, drugs, shopping, eating, gambling, …and the list goes on, seem to share with me one overarching addiction - *"our way thinking"*.

What do I mean by addiction to our thinking? Simply put, we just can't let "it" go. We get locked in on what we think - what we think about how things should go, how other people should act and react, even how we should feel about something or not feel at all. We become ensnared in our own thoughts about what 'good' means and what 'bad' means.

All of these thoughts I have found myself addicted to create a framework for life against which I judge. I judge how well my life is going. I judge the behavior of others. Based on the framework I've created for myself and the world around me, I can find myself judging everything and everyone. "This is good" or "this is bad". "This is right" or "this is wrong".

"My way of thinking" can lead to a great deal of heart ache. It can lead to unrest, uneasiness, resentment, anger, frustration, and so much more. For an addict or an alcoholic, it usually leads us to drink or use again if we can't get some freedom from it. For others it might lead to arguments with loved ones, hard feelings held for far too long, ruined relationships, or just a very difficult time wading through the events of life.

This book contains some stories of how I have been given, and have discovered, some incredible tools to deal with life exactly as it is and some Practices or Reflections at the end of each chapter to practice in daily life.

This is not a religious book, but it does contain spiritual practices. I'm perhaps not qualified to write about religious matters, but religion and spirituality are two distinct topics. I have no call to discuss anyone's belief or non-belief in God, Deity, souls or afterlife. I do however feel compelled to share the tools with which I find a spiritual freedom in this life – in this moment. "This moment" seems to be where we run into "problems".

Mind, spirit, or consciousness – these are the words we use to locate our dissatisfaction with life as it is, with him or her as they are, or to locate the fears that can lead us to make harmful decisions.

So many of us have experienced a brokenness of spirit whether we have a religious belief or not. I was broken on the inside, and I needed repair. Where I have sought a Spiritual Solution to my brokenness and where that Solution and I have come together to mend the cracks of my brokenness, are now some of the strongest parts of me.

I invite you to come along with me on a journey of spiritual awareness, expansion and greater understanding. I am 100% sure I am not unique. If this can work for me, it can work for you. Anything I can do you can do better.

# Chapter 1

---

## 1 - In the Beginning

I was lost. I was alone. I was out of answers. I had nowhere left to turn, and nothing left to do or say except, "help".

That was how I felt when I knew I was finished - finished drinking myself to death and finished trying to make my life work on my terms. This feeling was the key to a door - a door out of the hellish cycle of drinking and using drugs and into a life of freedom from the thoughts that took me back to the self-destructive behaviors that wrecked my life over and over again.

The title of this chapter is "in the beginning". It is the beginning of a journey into the depths of alcoholism and addiction and a prelude to the discovery of an incredible life on the other side. I would discover that so much of what I thought to be true about life, about myself, about the people around me was wrong - just wrong.

I don't know that anyone starts out with an intent to become an alcoholic or an addict. I didn't. I thought drinking was an adult thing to do. I thought it was glamorous. I thought it came with being fun, going to parties, being "popular". And it was fun. It was fun for a long time. Addiction is a very sneaky thing. For an alcoholic, or at least this alcoholic, it was fun until it wasn't. It was freedom until it became my prison. And, once the door to that prison closed, I wouldn't be able to open it again under my own power.

This is one of the elements of alcoholism that is so baffling to most of us. It doesn't make sense. This substance - this liquid - that once gave me the freedom to be the "me" I thought I was meant to be, eventually controlled me. The periods of fun became shorter and happened less often. The fun was eventually replaced with the pain of regret, shame and embarrassment. I kept chasing it though. I wanted alcohol to work like it did when I was younger.

I was fourteen years old when I started drinking. I remember that first drink like it happened just yesterday. I remember it so well because that first drink changed my life. I got drunk the first time I tried alcohol. And - it was amazing.

I had wanted to drink for a long time. I didn't want to because I knew what it was going to do to me or for me. I just wanted to. It was an adult thing to do. It was cool. It was forbidden.

It was made very clear to me that it was a sin to drink. It was a sin to even think about drinking. So, naturally I wanted to. I'm not sure where my obstinance came from. I seemed to have been born with it. If I wasn't supposed to do it, I felt it really needed to be done.

I was raised in one those families that had to make sure everything looked the way society thought it was supposed to look - in the Bible Belt. My family was ultra-religious - the fundamentalist, evangelical brand of religion. We weren't just religious. My family literally built churches - the buildings and the congregations.

We opened the doors for every church service. Everyone in the family was expected to be doing something in the church. My grandfather was a pastor. I had uncles that were pastors and traveling evangelists. If you weren't a pastor, you were at least teaching Sunday School. My mother did everything that church would allow a female to do. In my pre-teen years, my Saturday afternoons were spent straightening the hymnals and the literature kept in the trays on the backs of the pews.

Everything had to look just right – everything at church and everything at home. But the home-life reality did not match the image. We had a nice home. My brothers and I were provided for, materially. But there was a great deal of abuse.

My older brother and I were both mentally and physically abused as children, regularly. We each handled it in opposite ways. He tried to be the best little boy he could be. I went the other direction. The more I was abused the more rebellious I became. I think we both knew it was coming no matter how well we matched the template we were supposed to match.

I was a kid with a lot of insecurities and a lot of, what I later would find out were called, "resentments". I was convinced no one really wanted me around. I felt like my friends weren't really my friends. I was certain when people laughed near me they were laughing at me. My adolescent mind made up all of these stories about me and about my little world. It didn't matter then if the stories I told myself were true or not. If I thought them they were true to me.

I needed that first drink I took at age fourteen by the time I was ten.

So, when say it was amazing - it was amazing, magical, transformative - all the things a budding alcoholic like me needed it to be. I needed alcohol to get me through the life I was living until I could find the doors of recovery. It was the escape I needed - I really needed.

Alcohol did things for me I didn't know needed doing. I remember sitting in that park on a sunny, spring day in 1985. I remember how absolutely horrible 12-year-old scotch tasted when mixed with cola in a styrofoam cup. And I remember that first feeling of a "buzz".

It was incredible. I laughed. I laughed like I hadn't laughed before. I laughed hard - really hard. I talked - a lot. I couldn't, or wouldn't, shut up. I remember how green the grass was. I felt like I hadn't seen a green like that before. And the sky was blue - not the normal blue. This was a blue that made you exhale whether you needed to or not. It was a magical feeling. I wasn't just transformed – I was transported.

I wouldn't have said this at the time, I wouldn't have understood it if someone had said it to me; but what I was feeling was freedom. I was free from all of that pent up anger, resentment and fear. All the insecurity and feeling separate was gone. It just vanished.

I was with my three best friends in the park that day, but I felt closer to them than I'd ever felt before.

This is what alcohol does for an alcoholic like me. It didn't just make me feel good or great. It made me feel right. Alcohol did for me what I could not do for myself. I could drop my shoulders from my ears. I could smile and mean it. It altered my experience in this world in a way that not only made it bearable - I liked it. I loved it.

That's the first lie the disease of alcoholism told me. And I believed it.

The lie was that this was how I was supposed to feel. I felt so "right" it had to be the way I was supposed to feel. I needed it to be right. The next day I was sober again and I hated it. I was already making plans for my next drink - the weekend. I just needed to get to the weekend, and I knew I'd be able to do it again.

The weekend came. I got drunk again. I was happy again. I was at a party, and I could talk to anyone. I was fun *and* funny. People were coming up to me and talking to *me*. I was popular. There was nothing that fourteen-year-old boy wanted more. I had it and the price was easy to pay.

It wasn't long until I was drinking every day. At sixteen years old I would start my day with a few ounces of vodka in a few ounces of orange juice. This is the drink I would take into first hour Spanish class. I honestly didn't understand why other people weren't doing the same thing. Did they not know what this stuff was capable of? I had a buzz by 9:00 am and all was OK. I got an "A" in that class.

Drinking was working.

Off to college at the age of seventeen. Consequences started catching up to me. I wasn't going to class because I was too busy "having fun". I'm not sure I even knew where some of my classes were. I drank my way through both semesters of my freshman year. I didn't get to go back to that school for my sophomore year.

I learned from that experience that I needed to do enough to keep people off my back so that I could drink and party the way I wanted to. And I did. I started managing my drinking for the first time. Now it was something that needed to be managed.

Drinking was still working, but I was working harder to keep drinking.

I got through school and got married. I'd started my first career in law enforcement, and I was busy. I was busy with a marriage that was fast becoming a family. She became pregnant in our first month of marriage and our son was born nine months and sixteen days after our wedding day.

My career was taking more and more of my time. I drank less during this period. I would go weeks, or months, without drinking. I held on to that for years. I clung to the memory of not drinking for a few weeks or months in my early twenties as a reason why I wasn't really an alcoholic. This of course had no bearing on whether I was alcoholic or not. The disease of alcoholism is progressive. Left untreated, it only gets worse, never better.

The next few years were a whirlwind of change to say the least.

That marriage didn't last. Within a few years we were separated and then divorced. I was over-worked and burned out in that law enforcement career, so I changed careers at the same time.

Remember that ultra-religious upbringing? Well, that experience - it turns out - had repressed a pretty big part of me. About two years after our separation, I discovered I am gay. This realization unleashed a flurry of negativity hurled in my direction.

Within about eighteen months I had changed careers, came out, and due to being gay my relationship with my son was pretty much terminated (not a surprise in conservative Oklahoma in the 1990's), my family disowned me - and - I found gay bars. As a gay man in Oklahoma in the nineties, that was about the only place to be yourself and be safe at the same time.

Drinking started to turn on me. It was still fun, but I was starting to *need* it. I didn't need it to feel funny or popular as much anymore as I needed it to stop the self-loathing. I needed it to feel some kind of normal - or what became normal for me. Drinking was starting to take over. If something came between me and a drink, that thing wouldn't be around for long.

The more I drank the less room there was for anything else and the smaller my life became. The smaller my life became the more I needed to drink.

Then drinking wasn't enough. I started to cross lines I said I'd never cross. Cocaine? Sure. Ecstasy? Yeah, I'll try some. When drugs were stacked on top of drinking alcoholically, I was gone. My disease had taken me - all of me.

Within a couple of years, I was broke. I had a car, some clothes, a 19" TV that I had in college and that was it. I didn't have anywhere to live. But I had an answer: move. I moved from Tulsa, OK to Dallas, TX. This was my answer. In January 2004 I wound up in Dallas. I had $127 in my pocket and no job.

I knew one person in Dallas. I had his number in my flip phone. I flipped it open and called him. It was a Tuesday.

He answered.

I asked, "hey, what do you do on a Tuesday night?".

He answered, "we go to the Hideaway Bar".

I replied, "I'll see you there".

And, just like that I was drunk again that night.

One of the first "bumper sticker" messages we get in recovery is "nothing changes if nothing changes" another is "wherever you go, there you are".

Nothing about me had changed. I was still the drunk I'd been in Oklahoma. I was just in a new zip code and in a new bar. I brought me with me and there I was.

So, what happens to an alcoholic like me? I kept drinking. I slogged away at rebuilding a career. I kept drinking just about every day. I don't know how many times I went to work hungover or still drunk from the night before. I "captured" a boyfriend and kept him for a couple of years. It wasn't too hard. He drank the way I did. If you didn't drink like me, we weren't hanging out.

My life was becoming so small, but I didn't realize it. It was normal for me. I would go to work. I would go to happy hour which would then turn into drinks after happy hour which would then turn into a club and then the lights would come on…2:00am. I would be drunk and my alarm was going to be quite loud in four and a half hours.

On other nights I might find myself on the couch, a bottle or two of wine…the next thing I would know my alarm would sound in the bedroom. I would still be on the couch.

Wash, rinse, repeat.

This is where God comes into the story. Not the God I grew up with - the punishing, angry God that only likes you if you do everything exactly "right". This God is a God I learned about in my journey into and throughout my recovery. Some of us call it a Higher Power or Ultimate Reality or Spirit of the Universe. It turns out God doesn't really care too much what name we use. That seems to be our problem.

This God is caring, loving and apparently loves me just as I am. This God has an entire reservoir of grace waiting just for me. The only thing I ever have to do is turn to it and accept it.

In the summer of 2006, I was still in the "Wash, Rinse, Repeat phase" of my life. I set out one night to look for a coffee shop. I wanted a place that would be quiet so I could go there and get some work done in the evening. I knew if I stayed home, I'd be two bottles in and passed out.

I went from one coffee shop to the next getting farther and farther from home until I found one that looked good.

The parking lot was mostly empty. There were only four people inside. Four guys were sitting over in the corner talking, laughing and having a great time together. It was probably about eight o'clock at night. I would go back to this coffee shop again and again around the same time every night. Most nights they were there. We eventually started talking. I learned that they were there hanging out before a late-night meeting for recovery they would go to at 11:00 pm. This was interesting. They were interesting and fun to talk to. I didn't think too much more about it.

As it happened, I had tried coffee shop after coffee shop until I found the one coffee shop that was affectionately called "sober bucks" among people in the gay recovery scene in Dallas. I found this out after going earlier one day - right after work. I walked in at about 5:30 one evening and there must have been at least forty or fifty people in there. Some were paired up at tables going over what looked like homework. They had big, blue books opened up and some had notebooks open as well.

Some of them were just talking amongst themselves in what seemed to be some sort of code: "hey, are you going to the 6 or the 8?" "How many days do you have now?" "When are you picking up your chip?" I didn't know what any of this meant but if I was interested before, now I was downright intrigued.

I didn't know what was happening then, but I know now. Something Greater than me was working in my life. That Power greater than myself that I call God had somehow placed me right in the middle of gay recovery Mecca. I was surrounded. And I was soon to be hooked.

These people had something. I was falling in love with a whole group of people. They had some sense of ease, some sense of being that I hadn't been around before. These people were happy. They didn't drink. They didn't do drugs. And they still had fun. Gay people were having fun without alcohol or drugs.

Now, this is probably going to seem surprising. I still didn't know I had a problem with alcohol. I knew life wasn't all that great, but I didn't know it had anything to do with alcohol and certainly not alcoholism. I was really happy for these people - that they had found each other, and they had found a solution for their problem. I just really liked being around them.

It would take another two years for me to reach the point of saying, "enough". And the crazy thing is it didn't come at a point of some horrible, calamitous event (although I'd had many).

I had tried to stop drinking on my own. I counted days like I thought these people were doing. That didn't work. I tried just getting rid of all the booze I had at home. That didn't work. I tried saying

"I'm not going to drink tonight" to the people I was with. That might have lasted an hour into the night. That didn't work.

I was tired - tired of trying to manage my drinking and my life at the same time (neither with much success). It appeared these people had figured something out, so I finally asked one of them to take me to one of their meetings.

I was sure this was going to be the end of the life I was aiming for. Once you say you're an alcoholic you can't take that back. Right?

January 25, 2009, I said I was an alcoholic for the first time. It was an end and a beginning. It was the day I started my journey in recovery. And, like most journeys in life, this one hasn't been in a straight line. I've gone forward and backward and up and down.

I stayed sober for just about four years and relapsed.

We have some sayings that sound strange in recovery sometimes. Two of the sayings that sounded the most strange to me were: "I'm grateful to be an alcoholic" and "I'm grateful for the pain that brought me here".

I wouldn't really understand either of those sayings until getting sober again in January of 2015 - after a two-year relapse that took me to a complete spiritual void, homelessness and an attempted suicide.

How can anyone be grateful for all of that? I would find out in *the next chapter* of life.

## Finding Gratitude

First, you will need some paper and a pen or pencil. This is better done while actually writing and not done on a phone or computer.

Begin with either a prayer to your Higher Power or a simple expression of your intent to gain a clear understanding and a new experience. It might go something like this:

*"As I sit here, help me to see the true nature of things. Help me find the strength to see through my pain or discomfort in order to experience my own life, honestly. Remove from my perceptions any of the shades of sorrow, grief, anger, fear, resentment or loneliness."*

Once you've expressed an intent to sit with honesty, clarity and understanding, sit quietly for a few moments in a comfortable position. Think back to an experience you may have considered a "setback" or an experience you labeled as a "bad" event. This might be a lost job, a relationship that ended, a financial shortfall or even if you too have experienced a problem with alcohol or some other addiction and labeled these difficulties as "bad".

Now, start to write down some of the joyful or happy or beneficial events that came later – as a result of a hardship. I'll give some examples:

*Ended relationship with ___ :*

*I learned I was able to move forward on my own.*

*I had opportunity to spend more time with friends.*

*I had more time to devote to pursuits that were of more interest to me.*

*I was single and available when I was able to meet _____.*

*I learned that my self-worth was not tied to a connection with someone else.*

**Discovered and Admitted I am alcoholic:**

*Began to learn to accept help from others.*

*Was able to begin to build real self-esteem.*

*Relationships were repaired.*

*Was put on a path to emotional freedom and spiritual discovery.*

*Physical health was improved.*

Going back through my life and looking for the things to be grateful for – especially the things that came from a life event that I had labeled "bad" – has been transformative. It is a muscle that I can exercise. And over time it can become a working part of the mind. When I look for gratitude, I find it. When I live with gratitude, I live a happier and more contented life.

Hang on to this list. You might even want to start a notebook or journal to keep this work together in one place. When we get to chapter six we will begin to learn to fold our gratitude into a transformative daily practice.

## Chapter 2

---

## 2 - The Next Chapter

When I began my journey in recovery in January of 2009, I walked through the doors of my first meeting as a man who *thought* he *should* get sober. Unfortunately *thinking I should get sober* wasn't enough for me to completely surrender myself to a process of change required to grow spiritually and to stay sober.

In order to get and maintain sobriety, I would come to find out, the alcoholic or addict has to know - really know - they've reached the end of their drinking and using. I would have to know and admit to my innermost self that I couldn't go on like I had been. We have a catchy little phrase for that too: "Gift of Desperation".

In 2009 I knew I had a problem with alcohol. I knew I hadn't been able to stop drinking when I'd planned to. You might think that should be enough. It wasn't. But it was enough to get me through the doors of recovery for the first time. It was enough to open me up to the idea of recovery. And it was enough to put me in a place where I would be exposed to some of the ideas and concepts that would later save my life.

For four years I stayed in the rooms of recovery. I went to meetings. I went to dinners before and after meetings. I had hundreds and hundreds of conversations over hundreds and hundreds of cups of coffee. I held service positions in the groups I considered myself a member of. I *decided for myself* (not a great way for an alcoholic to begin a sentence) that all of this activity was going to be all I would need to stay sober. *I decided* this was keeping me sober and that this was all I needed to do.

I was wrong.

Getting and staying sober would require spiritual growth. It would require taking a good, hard look at where I've fallen short in my relationships - all of my relationships: home, romantic, professional, friends, random people on the street. I would have to look at how I showed up in the world and how I behaved. Spiritual growth would require a beginning. That beginning would entail getting a clear understanding of who I was - not who I thought I was. And it would require getting an understanding of what parts of *my* character were causing *my* problems. And any beginning in spiritual growth requires a spiritual connection - a connection to a Power great than myself.

Drinking again was going to be inevitable for me unless and until I became willing to do the work - the work of clearing the obstructions between God and me and then building a relationship with that Higher Power.

So, I drank again. And I went out with a bang. I didn't just sneak a drink somewhere. I threw a party - a big one. I bought boxes and boxes of wine, vodka, gin, tequila, whisky and mixers. I went out and bought new glassware so I would have just the right glass for whatever drink might be mixed or poured.

I had a big loft in a trendy area just east of downtown Dallas - over 80 feet of windows wrapping around my corner unit with a beautiful view. I don't remember how many people came to that party but there were quite a few people there. It was a great party in a perfect setting.

I got drunk. It didn't seem like a big deal at the time. I knew I was going to get drunk. I wanted to get drunk. I wanted to get drunk so that I could prove that getting drunk for me wasn't a big deal. (It's so difficult to write that sentence because the insanity just leaps off the page.)

Nothing bad happened that night. I got drunk - I had a good time. I was already home, so after the party I went to bed. I woke up the next day feeling different but OK. I felt oddly satisfied. But looking back I realize I felt alone again.

The next weekend I got drunk again. This time I went into a black out and "came to" in San Francisco. I'd been functioning in a black out for four days. I'd bought a plane ticket, gotten on a plane, traveled halfway across the country and continued to drink until I woke up in a hotel room by myself. This was a big deal.

I panicked. I didn't know where I was or how I got there when I woke up (aka "came to"). I had to piece together what I could of the previous few days and get back home. What story could I make up to cover my tracks? What could I say to the people at work? Then it hit me. I'd screwed up.

I knew right then that I shouldn't have left the rooms of recovery. I should have stayed.

I continued to drink for two more years. I found depths of alcoholism and addiction that I had never reached before. The more I drank the more alone I felt. It didn't matter if I was in a room full of people or sitting right next to my boyfriend at dinner with friends. I was still alone. No matter how much I drank I couldn't get back to that feeling I had when I started drinking. It used to make me feel some sort of happiness. Drinking used to tear down the walls that were between me and other people, but now it made them taller and thicker.

...left untreated, alcoholism only got worse - never better...

At the end of that two-year run, I was drinking all day every day. I drank in the morning, in the afternoon and throughout the evening. When I went to bed at night, I put bourbon or whiskey on the nightstand because when I woke up at two o'clock or three o'clock in the morning, I was going to need it to stop the shaking and maybe get another couple of hours of sleep.

I attempted suicide toward the end of 2014. I wrapped a belt around my neck and attached it to the top of a closet door. I lowered myself and waited. The belt broke. I fell to floor. I just sat there and cried. I've tried to put into words the utter, devastating aloneness and hopelessness that preceded that decision. I've never been able to find the words. That event led to being prescribed anti-depressants.

The medication helped - to a degree. But anti-depressants don't cure alcoholism. Another couple of months went by.

My Gift of Desperation came one Sunday afternoon. Driving down a street, I looked into the rearview mirror of my car just and said, "why doesn't life work anymore - why can't I make life work?". I've had horrible, catastrophic events in my life that could, or should, have caused me to reach this point. But it came when I was just empty - so empty.

I asked the question I didn't have an answer for; and God gave me a nudge.

In that moment, desperation and willingness came together - two prerequisites for me to begin a process of recovery. I made a decision. I was going to go back to recovery. I knew there was a "newcomer meeting" (meetings geared toward people new in recovery) Monday at 6:00pm. I was going to go to that meeting.

Hope returned. I'd felt hopeless for so long.

I started to feel a happiness again the instant I made that decision. My feeling of aloneness started to go away even though I was sitting alone in my car. I knew that group that I'd belonged to before was still there. I knew they had something that worked because most of those people were still there.

Miracles happen.

I went to bed that night, happy. I didn't put any bourbon on the nightstand that night. I slept all night, and I woke up happy. It had been months since I'd felt any kind of happiness or joy. I soon realized the feeling I'd had was a feeling of going home. I was going back to place of relief, of freedom - a place of safety and security.

This is how I can be grateful for the pain. All of that pain of feeling lost and alone, defeated and helpless led me to the door to freedom. All I had to do was be willing to open it and step through.

It's funny how some of the easiest things to do in life can seem so difficult - until we do them. Saint Teresa of Avila would say that obedience makes those things which seem impossible, possible. I would just substitute the word *willingness* for obedience.

I walked back into the rooms of recovery bankrupt - financially, emotionally and spiritually. That big loft was gone. No job. No money. That car I was in when I looked in the rearview mirror would soon go back to the bank. I had no place to live and "couch surfed" for the first few months of sobriety - sleeping on couches of friends or mattresses on floors. There were days I wasn't sure if or when I would eat. Some days it was a $1.79 burrito from a convenience store or maybe some tuna on crackers.

I was happy to be back, but I was terrified at the same time. I came back to the rooms of recovery completely desperate and completely destroyed. I woke up in fear and went to be in fear. I came back with an eagerness to recover - like my life depended on it. I finally knew and understood that my life depended on getting and staying sober. That knowledge and understanding is a true gift.

So, I began again. I found a sponsor in my first week back and started working the steps of recovery with him. We met weekly and he shared his experience with me. He shared his story with me and how his sponsor worked the steps with him. He showed me how to ask for help and to accept the help I had asked for. He taught me that asking for help didn't mean I was helpless - it meant I could be helpful. He helped me see the parts of me that were harming me that I couldn't see on my own. And he showed me a way to deal with the parts of my character that had become defective. He led me through a process of making amends for the harms I'd caused and showed me how to keep doing all of this as a way of life. He showed me a way of living that would lead to a sense of peace and serenity I hadn't known before.

Most importantly, he pointed me down a path of spiritual discovery. He told me that I was going to begin a relationship with God - the way I understand (or don't understand) God. He said this was the relationship that was going to carry me and sustain me through all life had in store for me - happy, sad, painful and joyful. And he told me that this relationship - it's formation, maintenance and growth - was my responsibility. I could have it - it was free.

And then we talked about my next responsibility - the responsibility to give it away. My responsibility as a person fortunate enough to have received this gift of desperation and this gift of recovery is to pass it on to the next seemingly hopeless, helpless alcoholic that walks through the door. This is how we keep our gifts. We give them away.

I learned that the spiritual world is not a zero-sum game. I found that my own spiritual experience grows when I give of myself – when I share my experience, my hope, the lessons I have learned along the way. When I give a piece of my spiritual pie to someone else, I don't have less pie. My pie gets bigger.

The expressed goal of the program of recovery I practice is to provide me with a spiritual awakening. Every step I take is designed to lead me in that direction. And here's the cool part: the destination isn't defined - just the direction - always forward, always growing even when the growth is seemingly imperceptible. I'm either moving toward a Power greater than myself or I'm moving toward a drink. I'm either growing in my spiritual experience in this life or I'm shrinking into my alcoholism. It's just that simple. My experience has proven it to me.

I would either have to "Grow or Go".

## A Practice of Beginning a New Thought

How do you form a new relationship? Or – if you have a relationship already, how do you renew it? A relationship with a Higher Power, or God, or Mystery, or Higher-Good – whatever words you can be comfortable with – is really no different than any other relationship. I have to share my life with the other party in the relationship. I speak – AND – I listen. I'm honest. I'm giving of my time. I ask for help when I need it, and I'm humble in receiving the help that is offered.

I know a lot of us fall out of practice with prayer, if we ever had a practice at all. For those of us that have never had a practice, beginning may seem awkward or even pointless. I know I fell squarely in the "this feels awkward" group. Luckily, the practice I'll be outlining here is done solo – so there's no need for any feelings of awkwardness or embarrassment.

Beginning is the hardest part. So, let's make this simple.

First, arrange a few minutes of alone time in the morning. It can be as few as five minutes in the beginning.

Second, find a quiet place for this morning quiet time where you can sit comfortably.

Third, when your morning time comes, just sit there with your eyes closed. Sit in the quiet – no music, no cell phone, no TV – just silence.

Take a few breaths and just try to be there. Feel the floor under your feet and the chair under your body. Be aware of the air around you.

Fourth, say to yourself something like: "I surrender to this moment exactly as it is". Sometimes people feel a little tinge of anxiety just by expressing this thought. That's OK. This is a foreign concept to many of us and our egos would prefer we not surrender to any moment but rather try to manage it.

Fifth, express either verbally or in your mind, something like "Higher-Good please direct my thoughts and my actions today. Please help me to see the truth of each situation and find understanding and compassion in each moment".

Sixth, remain in silence for a few moments to take in all of what you just expressed. The silence is where we make space for a new thought. We need to practice so that we can become comfortable with silence.

In each of the points above, we are beginning to surrender to a new way, a new process of thinking, a difference perspective, and a new course of action. We are beginning to surrender our old way of acting and reacting to a new way of acting and reacting out of our highest potential.

This is a beginning – setting the groundwork for growth.

## Chapter 3

---

## 3 - Grow or Go

"Grow or go"…sounds like something some unhappy curmudgeon might bark out from the back of the room. But it isn't. No one has ever said this to me as a directive. It's just a reality in recovery. I'm either going to *grow* or I'm going to *go*. This has been my own experience and it's been what I have witnessed having been on this journey for fifteen years now.

I heard an old-timer say once, "The winners are those alcoholics who have found a way to be happy and sober at the same time. That's it. It doesn't have anything to do with what you've got, where you live or who your friends are." That guy is a good friend of mine now and is closing in on fifty years of sobriety as I write this.

When my two-month-sober brain heard that, I perked up. I really wanted to know how to be sober and be happy at the same time. I was still living in quite a bit of fear. My life was still in shambles. I still didn't have a job. I still didn't have any money. I didn't know where or how I was going to live. I only knew I didn't want to drink, and I was willing to do whatever it took. I knew I was happy to be sober, but I really hoped that wasn't as far as it would go for me.

I began to learn what happiness is. This was yet another thing I had wrong. I had happiness confused with jubilance or some sort of exuberant joy. Over the next few months, I would begin to redefine what happiness means for me. Happiness came to mean a sense of peaceful contentedness.

That may not sound like much to a non-alcoholic, but *peaceful* and *content* are not native feelings for us. We, generally, are ill-at-ease people prone to discontent. This peaceful contentedness I would find would be a direct result of a relationship with a Power greater than me.

As I said in the last chapter, my sponsor was taking me through the work necessary to remove the obstacles between me and my ability to build a relationship with the God *of my understanding*. We then began having conversations about what a relationship with God might look like. We started talking about prayer and meditation.

Prayer, I knew about, and I thought I knew about meditation. It turned out I didn't know much about either. My experience with prayer had always been to make a list of things I needed God to do for me and then communicating that list to God, in a very polite way, with an appropriate "amen" at the end. I had never meditated but was sure I knew what that was about too - incense, sitting on mats, maybe a mantra for good measure.

My ideas needed to be replaced with some new ideas.

First, I had to stop trying to talk God into doing the stuff I wanted God to do. Alcoholics are terribly self-centered people, so I had to begin a relationship with God on a new basis. My new goal was to be other-centered or God-centered. Rather than trying to talk God into my plans I was going to start asking God for his plans for me and the power or strength to carry those plans out. (forgive the male pronoun - I believe God is without gender but I needed a pronoun.)

It's amazing how short prayers can become when I simply ask God to direct my thinking.

I started praying this way. I started trying to speak to God in a way that put God in charge and left me out of the planning business. To continue to ask God for all the stuff I want to have happen would be to leave my ego center-stage. And, when my ego is front and center it's nearly impossible for me to put others first or to think of others first. When my ego is first, my world remains a place where it's all about me and what I want. This is not a framework for any sort of spiritual growth.

This simple shift in focus opened up an entirely new experience for me with God and with the people around me. I was no longer focusing on what I was getting or wasn't getting. I began, slowly, to see other people and their experiences. I began to see other people as myself and myself in other people. And I started to learn how to put the needs of other people before my own.

Then I realized the strangest thing had happened. I wasn't so worried about myself as much anymore. While I was busy praying for God's will in my life, my life started to change. I got busy doing the work and my perspective changed. I was able to begin putting one foot in front of the other and to move through life with some degree of grace.

I was staying sober. A day turned into a week. Then I was sober for a month and then two months. The days and weeks were stacking up. I remember walking into a convenience store about two months into sobriety to get something to eat. I got the food, probably a cheap burrito, and left. When I got outside, I realized I'd walked right by an open cooler of beer in ice right next to the checkout counter. It didn't even phase me. I walked right past it as if it had been loaves of bread on a shelf.

I had tears in my eyes as I walked away from that store. I knew this thing was working. I knew I was in the right place and doing the right things. That one tiny event - walking past the beer - was enough to propel me forward.

My material world began to follow my spiritual growth.

As I continued in sobriety and continued trying to do my best - to the best of my ability on any given day - I started to do a little better financially. I got a job. I kept that job. I got an apartment. I kept that apartment. I got a car and paid for it. I got some furniture to put in that apartment. My mattress was put on a bed frame, and I had a TV on a TV cabinet.

I still had one very healthy fear though - the fear of drinking again. I've seen it happen so many times - someone comes into recovery with their life burning down around them. They get a little sober time under their belt. Life gets a little easier to live. The heat comes off and out they go - back to drinking. I'd gone out before, and it nearly killed me. I couldn't let that happen again.

This "Grow or Go" saying always comes back to me.

My sponsor and I had been talking about prayer and meditation. I'd been praying - praying was easy. I didn't know how to meditate though. I didn't even really know what it meant to meditate. The literature in the program of recovery to which I belong is, frankly, a bit vague on the subject. But I knew I needed to do it. Our literature is clear on one aspect - I'm supposed to be doing it. The way we improve our conscious contact with our Higher Power is through a practice of prayer and meditation.

My sponsor asked me again one day how my meditation was going. I told him it wasn't *going*. I finally just asked him what I was supposed to be doing for meditation, "I don't know how." He said, "it's easy, you just start meditating and then keep doing it".

My internal dialogue kicked in: "what the hell does that mean?".

I now know that he was sending me on my own errand. He told me early on that my relationship with God was my responsibility. He wanted me to seek. He wanted me to take the initiative to go find the thing that was going to work for me. He wasn't going to spoon feed me. I wasn't going to grow, the way I needed to grow, being spoon fed.

So, I started seeking. One of the most important lessons I've learned in recovery is that the learning is in the seeking, not in the finding. In the seeking is where I've found the most joy.

By about three months sober I was meditating regularly. It wasn't easy, mostly because I still didn't really understand this meditation thing. But I was doing it. I would wake up in the morning, have some coffee, and sit quietly. Sometimes I would read something with some spiritual significance and think about what I'd read and how it might apply to me or what it meant to me. Sometimes I would ask God a question and then journal what I thought God might say or how God might answer.

The important thing was that I was starting my day with some time spent with my Higher Power. This time was an expression of my intent to do things God's way that day rather than my own – or to make my way match God's way. I knew this was going to be a necessary part of my day if I was to stay sober and free from the self-defeating thoughts that seem always to be waiting for me.

This was enough to start with. Just that much was a dramatic shift from the way I was living just a few months earlier. My life had been spent trying to make the world conform to my will. It's no surprise that this exertion of my will on the world led to a consistent state of frustration, unhappiness, and resentment.

A new way of living was taking the pressure off of me to make the world spin around the sun and somehow make everything work out just right. I was learning moment by moment, day by day to let things happen as they happen; to take stock of my own activities, actions and reactions; and to try to make an accurate appraisal of how I'm showing up in the world around me.

I was changing. I wasn't very aware of it at the time, but we rarely are, in the moment. My trajectory usually only becomes visible to me when I get some distance. Looking back, I can see where I've grown and where I haven't. My "growth line" might look like a graph line on the stock exchange - full of ups and downs with a trendline that somehow always moves upward.

Perspective is important. Part of growing up in sobriety is learning to being able to observe my own life with some objectivity.

I spent a lifetime going through life as the person things happened to. Eventually, I could become the person that observes the things that happen.

I began to see that growth takes work - and continued work. It would be like watering a garden. I can't just water it once and walk away. I must continue to water the seeds.

# A Practice - Beginning the Relationship

Some of us have or have had issues with an idea of "God". Some of us haven't. It was very important for me, when beginning this journey, to at least be open to a *loving* God. The notion of God I group up with wasn't going to work anymore. And, frankly, I now believe that conception to be incredibly harmful.

What if God was actually loving? What if God was going to accept me, care for me, and continue to love me regardless of my shortcomings? What if God saw me as created from love in order to love?

This is the God I have found on my journey – non-judgmental, accepting, loving, caring. This is the God I rest with and sit with. This is the God that comforts me in times of sadness, supports me in times of difficulty, and smiles back at me when I smile at creation. This is the God that has given me strength and direction to get sober, stay sober and try to help someone else.

Where is a good place to start?

We're going to be writing some more. Get out your notebook and pen or pencil again.

We're going to write a letter to Love. This is the Love of God – the Love that is God – the God that is Love.

In your letter, ask any question you would ask a loving God. I asked in a letter to God once where he'd been. I asked why I had to be alcoholic. I asked why my family disowned me and why I was then going through life alone. Ask this Love anything you want to ask and say to this Love anything you want to say. There are no rules.

Then write a letter back to yourself from that Love – from pure Love. Before you begin sit quietly. Start to imagine what pure Love might feel like. Where does that much Love come from? Imagine if you were surrounded by it – embraced by it. What would the most loving God say back to you? How would this loving God reply?

I like to do this because this is the voice we can begin to listen for. It is in every one of us. This loving, non-judgmental, perfectly supportive voice is the voice that is available to guide every single one of us. It is the voice, born in love, that knows the right thing to do, the right way to respond, the way to show up for ourselves and for those around us.

This is the beginning of a new relationship with God or Mystery or Higher-Good or the Universe. A relationship in which we speak, ask – AND - listen.

Chapter 4

## 4 - Watering the Seeds

What does it mean to water the seeds? *'Watering the seeds'* is a line I received from my Buddhist practice. *Watering the seeds* refers to diligence – diligently picking up the spiritual tools that bring about right thinking, right speech and right action. In this chapter, I'll be speaking primarily of the thoughts we have, the thoughts we engage in and how we can take action on a daily basis to water the seeds in our consciousness we choose to water. A seed could be a positive seed of understanding, compassion, loving kindness, etc. Or, that seed could be a negative seed of judgment, anger, jealousy, fear, discrimination, etc.

Imagine your consciousness having two parts: *store consciousness* and *mind consciousness.* In the store consciousness, all of the emotions and feelings of which we are capable are stored. When the seeds of those feelings and emotions are watered and fed, they grow up and into our mind consciousness.

Our mind consciousness is what governs or dictates our thoughts and actions. So, when we water the seeds of anger and resentment, anger and resentment grow in our mind and inform our thoughts and actions. When we water the seeds of loving kindness and compassion, those feelings inform our thoughts and actions. The longer and more consistently we water any seeds the more they grow, the stronger they become and the deeper their roots grow.

***

In order to live a happily sober life, I need to actively do something to nourish the positive seeds in my consciousness. That is to say, I need to do something on a daily basis to activate acceptance, compassion, empathy, kindness, understanding, etc., and become less self-centered. To be less self-centered I need to become more other-centered or more God-centered. This isn't something I can just pray for in the morning and then launch into the world with the same patterns or direction of thought I've always had. I would need to find a way for my thinking to be changed - the thinking that chooses my words and actions.

Every morning, I need to wake up, spend time with God in silence, and *water the seeds* I already have of *doing the right thing*. Taking time each morning with the expressed intent to connect to that little voice inside that already knows the right thing to do and to use that voice to guide my decision-making and my actions would be a life-changer for me on this journey through a sober life.

This isn't to say I never did the right thing before. But, given the option of doing what I knew to be right or doing what I really wanted – even when I knew it was the wrong thing to do - I would do what I really wanted nearly every time.

A self-centered life is pretty much all the alcoholic really knows. We tend to run our lives based on fear. Fears of not getting what we want, or what we think we need, or fears of losing what we have, send us out into the world wreaking havoc in our own lives and the lives of those around us. Our behavior may appear so ludicrous to someone paying attention that they may think we're *trying* to ruin our lives. These fears drive us to be self-centered: "if I'm not looking out for what I need to happen, who's going to make it happen?".

Faced with the fact that my life lived on my power would be continually wrecked by this crippling self-centeredness, I came to terms with one of the great facts of recovery from any addiction. I would need to tap into some Power greater than my own self-will that could bring about a change in me and give me the strength to keep going.

Tapping into, and staying tapped into, this Power greater than myself is the journey. 'Tapping into' is the beginning. 'Staying tapped into' is the *watering*. A practice of sitting quietly with God and touching those seeds of understanding, compassion, empathy, joy, insight, etc. keeps me in-touch with and gives me access to the ground of my being – the "me" I'm meant to be or rather who I already am when my Higher-Good isn't over-shadowed by my own ego-driven self-seeking thinking and behavior.

One of the bedrock tenets in my program of recovery is to *continue*. These principles, or steps, I am to practice don't get put up on a shelf and left there. I am to bring them into my life as a daily practice. They become the way I live my life. And, if someone can be successful at this even half of the time, amazing transformation can begin to take place. One of these principles includes prayer and meditation.

When I was about six months sober, I came across this method of meditation, or contemplation, called Centering Prayer. I had been scouring the internet looking for a meditation practice that could take me deeper than the "make it up as I go along" plan I'd been using. That plan had worked well enough in the earliest part of my beginning, but I knew there was more out there. And I knew I was going to need it.

One night I found an old video on YouTube that looked like it had been recorded on a VHS camcorder in the nineteen-eighties. The video had a Trappist monk giving a lecture. He was talking about a method of contemplation rooted in the ancient Western tradition but that had been updated for contemporary practitioners.

He described this extremely simple method of sitting comfortably in a chair. The person practicing should sit quietly, eyes closed, and have in mind one simple word. This word would be used to express the intent to consent to the presence and action of God within. The word wasn't used repeatedly like a mantra - just kept in reserve in case some thoughts came to mind that were just too interesting to let go of.

The simplicity really grabbed me. I think I knew on some level that any method I would engage in would need to be simple and easy to implement if I was to make it a part of my daily life. So, I started.

I wrote down the instructions as Father Keating gave them. I decided on my word - a *sacred word* or *word of intent*. The word wasn't sacred on its own. My word of intent would simply mean what I needed it to mean in the context of my meditation. I chose the word *Peace*. Peace was and is something I value about as highly as I value anything today.

I sat down for my first experience with Centering Prayer. I got quiet and settled into my chair. I said a short little prayer to myself. I introduced my word - and ZOOM! There went my brain. It seemed like it was producing chatter like never before. Thoughts, memories, internal dialogue, images, sounds - I was thinking thoughts I didn't even know I was thinking. This wasn't the experience I was hoping for.

Then I remembered another part of that lecture: my brain is supposed think. I'm not going to stop it. If it stops thinking, we have a problem. This is what the word is for. And I can use the word a thousand times if I need to.

Father Keating relayed a story in one of the talks I saw at some point. He was teaching the method to a group of nuns. After the portion of the class when Centering Prayer was practiced, one of the sisters came up to him. She said, "Father I'm terrible at this. I just don't think I can do it. I must have had 10,000 thoughts during our sit". He simply replied, "Sister, how wonderful! 10,000 opportunities to return to God".

That story pretty much sums up a practice of meditation or contemplation. It's a *turning* to God. In turning to God, a*s I understand God*, I let go of my own thoughts, agendas and ideas in exchange for an experience with God. It's a surrender to the Presence. Meeting God in the present moment in an attempt to be free from myself and to be free to participate in Ultimate Reality. *Turning* and *Letting Go* are two major themes in contemplative life.

So, I did it again, and again and again. I began to develop a regular practice of quiet time in the morning with God. And after a couple of weeks my five-minute meditation became eight and then ten and then fifteen minutes. Within a few weeks I was doing twenty minutes every morning.

Twenty minutes a day can change your life. It started changing mine.

One of the first benefits I remember experiencing was this sense of overall calm. The things that used to bother me or get on my nerves weren't bothering me as much anymore. They did at times of course, but not as much.

As I went on, I found this practice of *letting go* of thoughts in my periods of meditation was carrying over into my daily life. My ability to just let go of stuff was getting stronger. Very often it would happen without having to make a conscious effort to do it. It just happened.

Spending time every morning with the expressed intent of trying to do better, trying to be better, was working. Eventually, I would begin to want to be more understanding and more compassionate. I would begin to want to act out of love rather than fear. This practice of *turning to God* and learning to *let go* was helping me to let go of all those old ideas of trying to make happen the things I decided I needed to happen.

I began to intentionally water the positive seeds of understanding, compassion, empathy, and kindness.

Now, I haven't become some angel by any means. No one is handing out halos at any of the doors I've gone through. But I can say I like the person I am today. I enjoy being able to remind myself to be understanding when I find I am not. I like reminding myself to find ways to be kind.

As I continued to practice, I continued to reap the benefits. And quite honestly, if there weren't benefits, I probably wouldn't be doing it. I've found meditation, or contemplation, to be very practical in my own experience. I was told it would be, but I still had to experience it for myself before I really believed it.

I started developing this real and somehow tangible relationship with the God of my understanding (even though my understanding was that I didn't understand). I began looking forward to my mornings. There were times when I would wake up late in the first few months and rush out into the world without my quiet time with God. My days were noticeably different when this happened.

Luckily, I can get quiet for at least a couple of minutes just about anywhere to reinforce that connection. My *word of intent* can be used anytime and anywhere. If I'm feeling a little disconnected, I can stop, breathe, introduce my word and touch the positive seeds in my consciousness. I can close my eyes, let go of everything around me, and be opened to a new experience.

When I want to feel close to God, I don't have to *do* anything. I just need to *stop doing*.

For nine years now I've been *watering the seeds* in the hope of growing a relationship with God. My practice has grown. My relationship has grown.

Today, I know where to go when I feel troubled or just a little "off". I know where God is and all I have to do is turn to that place. God is always in the same place. The place is within me, and the moment is the *Now*.

When anxiety hits or fear creeps in I stop and come back to my home. My home is *Now*. Wherever I am I can stop, breathe in, breathe out, turn to the Presence of God within and say quietly to myself *Peace*. This has become my default reaction to stressful situations. It's my default because I have continued to practice. What began as a hit-or-miss five-minute practice has grown into a way of life for me. I have been able to water the seeds. They have grown roots that continue to strengthen and grow deeper.

# A Practice of Meditation

Silence is the space I make for a new idea to enter. Silence is the environment in which I can begin to become the observer of my thoughts. In the silence, I can begin to hear the whisper of the guiding voice within. As I become accustomed to listening for that voice and hearing it – through practice – this voice of Higher-Good can become clearer and more easily accessed.

Below are some easy-to-follow instructions for Centering Prayer, as I practice it. Some call this a prayer of quiet or contemplative prayer or simply meditation. It is merely a method through which I can train my mind to become comfortable in repose. In practicing, I can slow down my reactions and make time for a choice. And over time I can become better acquainted with the "true me" underneath the ideas of me and the self-images I have created for myself.

**First**, find a place to sit comfortably for a few minutes in the morning. This is best done in the morning soon after getting up. I wake up and have about half a cup of coffee and then begin. The goal is twenty minutes, but you might start with three or five minutes if you have a mind as busy as mine was when I began. The important thing is just to begin. We can add more time to our "sit" as we progress.

**Second**, choose a word with one or two syllables to use as an expression of your intent to sit in the Presence. Your word doesn't have to mean anything special in and of itself. Some people use a word such as: peace (this is the word I use), still, trust, yes, smile… it can be any word you choose. Some people like to use words with religious connotations, such as: God, Father, Jesus, Yeshua, Abba, Mother, etc. Whatever word is comfortable for you. The only thing we don't do is change the word during our "sit". We can choose a different word for next time, but just don't change it in the middle. Some people prefer to use a breath instead of a word. Of course this works too. But it is easier, in the beginning at least, to use a word. Trust me on this.

**Third**, sit quietly with eyes closed and silently (in your mind) introduce your word. We close our eyes in order to let go of everything around us. The only effort we expend during our quiet time is the reintroduction of our word - IF - we find ourselves pulled into our thoughts. A thought in the context of this meditation is anything happening in our mind – a thought, an image, a memory, plan-making, internal dialogue, etc.

To have a thought is perfectly normal. Example: "I'm hungry" is a thought. Having that thought is fine. We just don't get swept up in that thought.
Example: "I'm hungry. I wonder what's for lunch. I hope it isn't meatloaf again." – this is being pulled into thought.

If we find ourselves caught in thought, we reintroduce our word as easily and effortlessly as possible – imagine laying a sleeping baby down so as not to wake her – softly, gently. We don't use our word in frustration. Remember, a functioning brain is supposed to think – it is supposed to be active. When we realize our mind has been drawn into thought (because this will happen) we're just going turn from our thoughts back to the Presence. Our word of intent is the vehicle for that turning. When we use our word of intent it redirects our attention to our original intent of sitting with the Silence and we let go of our thoughts so they can just float by.

This is the purpose. We are training our minds to witness our thoughts. We are training our minds to be able to release thoughts – to let them go. This is a process of ***letting go*** and ***turning to***.

Over time, our word of intent may disappear altogether. It becomes a part of our subconsciousness. Eventually, we subconsciously release our thoughts - let them go in order to remain in the Silence. This takes different amounts of time for different people. It might be a year or three years or more. (It doesn't really matter if it disappears at all.) It has mostly disappeared for me after nine years, but there are days when I use my word about every 30 seconds it seems. It's all fine. Remember the story from Father Keating: "10,000 opportunities to return to God". Any time spent practicing "letting go" is time well-spent.

**Fourth**, at the end of our "sit", we remain in silence for a couple of minutes in an effort to bring the Silence into the day with us. We're not using our word during this time. We're just being quiet. Let the silence surround you and bring it into your day. Take it out into the world with you.

I said in the beginning to begin with just three or five minutes if you need to. This is fine, but remember we need to get to at least twenty minutes. So, starting with five minutes is perfectly acceptable. After a day or two add a couple more minutes. As you get more comfortable sitting in silence, adding two or three more minutes every few days won't be difficult. Hold yourself accountable. No one else can.

**_Twenty minutes a day will change your life._**

# Chapter 5

## 5 - A God of Our Understanding

I have been using, and will be using, the word "God" and the phrase "God, *as I understand God*" quite a bit throughout this book. And I've touched briefly on what I mean by this in earlier chapters. But now that I'm talking about a relationship with this *God of my understanding* it might be beneficial to put down on paper a little more about what this phrase means.

First, the word "God". This isn't the only word I use to refer to this Power. Anytime you see words like *Presence, Power, Ultimate Reality, Mystery, Great Reality, Spirit of the Universe, Higher Power, Higher-Good, etc.,* …any words like this that are capitalized, I'm using these as a name for the God of *my understanding*.

Something I'm very grateful for is the ability to think of God the way I need to think about God. This isn't meant to offend anyone, but the God I grew up with, in the church I grew up in, was a very small God. He (male pronoun used intentionally here) was tyrannical. He was angry most of the time. He was punishing. Sure, he was given credit for creating all of creation, but he sure wasn't very happy with what he created. The only way that God was really going to love me was if I did everything exactly right - one unforgiven slip and into the hellfire I would go.

This wasn't an idea of God I could believe in as I began a process of learning to rely on God. It certainly wasn't an idea I could believe in after living a life in meditation and contemplation for any amount of time. To sit with that much love - what I experienced to be unconditional love - meant that my idea of God had to grow, to expand.

What I have discovered over the years is that the less I think about what God is, the better off I am. I have discovered that the things that most often come between me and God are what I think about God, what I think this Power will or won't do, where I think The Ultimate Mystery is or isn't, what I think the Universe likes or doesn't like, etc. The truth is I just don't know.

"I don't know" is a wonderful answer to the question "what is God?".

I do know that anything I think of God is less than God is. No matter how many attributes I might assign to God I can never fully describe all that God is. I can only experience what I have been opened to and reach for what I hope to find. I walk and observe, and if I'm open to seeing the Presence, I will see it everywhere – everywhere I have been, anywhere I am, and anywhere I am going.

I heard someone say once, "I don't know what God is, I just know *that* God is. 'God is' is a complete sentence". That line resonated so deeply with me because I don't know what God is. I just know that God is. Trying to figure God out is a task too great for me. I heard someone else say once, "you're going to get a spiritual hernia trying to figure God out".

I've begun and nurtured a relationship with this Mystery that gives me strength to make new choices - choices that perhaps I wasn't even aware of before. I've developed a relationship with a God that doesn't pardon me from life but sustains me in all of life's challenges. I still get to live all that life has in store for me – all of it.

I have a relationship with God today that blankets me in peace. This Power provides a sense of serenity in situations that at one time would've sent me spinning off. The Ultimate Mystery is the calm sense of surrender at the very center of my being where I can rest and find solace.

My finite brain will never be able to grasp the infinite. But I do know what my experience has been. My experience has been that the more I rely on God, the more easily my life goes. The more I lean on God, the more easily I'm able to deal with life on life's terms. The deeper my practice goes, the more clearly I can hear the *still small voice* within. The more closely I live with God the more gratitude I have for all the life I have lived and the life I am currently living. And the more I turn over to God the more of God I get to experience.

For an alcoholic like me to have gratitude for all I have experienced is no small feat. If I know anything at all, I know a relationship with the God of my (or your) understanding and even an ounce of gratitude can transform.

## A Practice of Looking for God

When I start looking for something, there it is. Did you ever buy a car and then all the sudden start seeing cars on the road just like the one you bought? Never really noticed that many before but there they are. Or how about looking for someone through a crowd and suddenly there are so many people that look like the person you're looking for?

When I started looking for the Presence of God, the same thing happened for me. Everywhere I looked there was evidence of something way beyond the power of human power. What would happen if God stopped "Godding" or Nature stopped "Naturing" or Science stopped "Sciencing"? (I know I just made up three words there.) How much would cease to be? How much would be forgotten, how many feelings would go unrealized, or emotions evaporated, or what love would be undone?

I was watching a nature show on TV not too long ago and they were talking about how baby sea turtles come to be. The mother turtle comes on shore, burrows into the beach sand and lays the eggs. She covers the eggs and back out to sea she goes. When the eggs hatch, the baby turtles make their way to the surface, scurry as fast as they can to the water, and swim out to sea. They even do this most often at night to avoid predators. No one told the baby turtles to do this. No mama turtle gave instructions. She wasn't even there for them to follow. They just knew. There was something in them that already had the instructions.

Ducks know to fly south. They know how to make formations to make the long flight easier to complete.

Our bodies know how to reproduce skin cells to repair damage and to replace the cells we lose as a course of living.

Our minds know how to love. I only have to think of seeing my son for the first time to know what love is. We know love in so many ways, and it just happens. Whether it be a significant other, a child, a parent or grandparent, or a pet – a dog or a kitten, most of us have felt love for someone. No one taught us how to feel love, how to manufacture it, how to make it happen – because we can't manufacture it or make it happen. It is a gift that has been given and it is inside us. We already have it.

So, here is our practice. We are going to begin a practice of awareness.

**First**, take out that pen and paper again. Sit quietly for a few minutes and just fall into the moment. Close your eyes and let go of everything around you. Let go of your worries and concerns for a few minutes.

**Second**, begin to bring to mind places or events or instances when you can see or have seen a Power beyond human power working in your life. Bring to mind examples of a Power greater than human power that you've witnessed in nature, in relationships, in whatever sense they come to you. Sit there and let your mind go.

**Third**, start to write them down. I think you'll be surprised how the pace of these thoughts quickens after a moment or two.

**Fourth**, think about this: why would we be any different? We are creations in this world just like everything else. If God, or Nature, or whatever word you feel comfortable with, would give a turtle their instructions, or a duck, or the waves in the ocean, or the moon orbiting the earth, or the tiniest little skin cell, why wouldn't there be instructions for us too? There is in me, and in you, the voice that says, "this is right and that is wrong", "I should go this way, not that way", "It is better to love than hate", "it is better to act out of love than anger".

Make this a regular practice. Just take a few moments throughout the week. (Put it on your calendar if you need to.) As you make this a practice in your life, you will (as I have) begin to see this Power at work – everywhere and all the time.

Life is still life. People still make bad decisions. People are born and people pass on. There is harm and pain and all of the uncomfortable parts of living a life. There is also happiness and joy and peace and love. We get to live it all. I am consistently reminded that this Power sustains us through all life brings just as this Power sustains all of everything.

I am not excused from life, but I am supported, held and loved…this Truth is as true for you as it is for me.

# Chapter 6

## 6 - Gratitude Transforms

Gratitude is indispensable. It seems to be the one thing, when all else fails, that can turn my whole attitude around.

I wrote in earlier chapters about the state of my financial, mental and emotional well-being when I came back into the rooms of recovery. In the earliest days of sobriety, I went to bed at night submerged in fear. When I woke up in the morning, I was swimming in dread - or perhaps just treading. I was terrified of drinking again and had no idea how anything in my life was going to "work out".

It would have been easy for me to stay in self-pity and self-loathing in those circumstances, but for an alcoholic seeking recovery that really isn't an option. I found some hope to hang onto in the fellowship I found in recovery. Eventually, though, hope needs to be transformed into some faith or belief. I need to *believe* that on some level - any level - things will be OK.

But what does *OK* mean? This is one of the first definitions I had to look at from a spiritual perspective.

I don't know if finding a way to be grateful for *just what I had* made what I had OK - or if deciding what I had was sufficient *for today* made space for gratitude to creep in. It's one of those "chicken and egg" scenarios for me. I don't really know which came first but I do know they go hand in hand. Either way (and I don't think it really matters) gratitude began to change my entire mindset.

I noticed one day a feeling gratitude for whatever food I had for that day - no matter how repetitive it was or whether that was what I really wanted to eat or not. When I became grateful for one more $1.79 burrito, I no longer resented having to eat one more $1.79 burrito. When I became grateful for someone giving me a ride to a meeting, that gratitude supplanted some of the self-pity of not having my own transportation.

Gratitude is something that spreads too. When I use it as a tool, and not just a feeling, it can edge its way into more and more areas of my life.

I started *using* gratitude in my daily life when I noticed it working. I would wake up in the morning and thank God for a new day to live sober. I would ask God to direct my thinking - that it be free from my will and aligned with His. And I would sit quietly with a simple intent to be with God and begin to try to listen to the voice in me that knows better.

Gratitude started making life easier to live. When I began to live more easily, I could make decisions more easily. I could begin to see the next steps to take - the very next action in front of me.

In about my sixth month of sobriety I got an email from a large rideshare company. They had a plan for people to start driving for them and to lease a car through their company as part of the deal. It was an expensive lease, but it was a car AND a job. I jumped on it. It was perfect for me, and it was easy to get started. I filled out the forms, got approved, went down to the dealership, and picked up a new 2015 Ford Fusion. I started driving for them the next day.

Suddenly I was making money, and I had my own transportation to meetings. This form of work gave me the flexibility to work when I needed to (which was a lot) and to take breaks for all the meetings I wanted to go to. I was able to make just enough money to meet my financial needs and had the time available for my spiritual needs and my service commitments. It was perfect.

I needed gratitude to outweigh my pride. I had been a partner in the firm I was with prior to my "downfall". I had made a lot of money once upon a time. And I was very proud of all the professional accomplishments I had achieved.

There I was driving for a rideshare company and grateful for it. I had established a _practice of gratitude_. Don't get me wrong - I could still feel embarrassed. But I wouldn't, couldn't, allow myself to stay in that feeling. I had a real fear of picking up someone I'd worked with or someone that I had known at the height of my career, but I couldn't allow myself to be ruled by those fears. All I had to do was remember where I was before this job and gratitude was able to sweep in.

When I make space for gratitude, gratitude appears. I remember getting enough money to buy ground coffee so I could make my own coffee in the morning. I started my day with scoops of gratitude. Quite a few years have passed since then, and I still think of that feeling sometimes when I'm buying coffee or setting the timer for the coffee maker for the next morning. Looking for places to be grateful and even the smallest things or events to be grateful for is a substantial part of my practice today.

As time has gone on my life has gotten back to what might be considered "normal" - although I hesitate to use that word. When I was about three years sober, I started a new firm with a former colleague. My professional life has rebounded in a way that has given me a tremendous amount of flexible time to devote to recovery. I am back in the profession I was in prior to hitting my bottom in alcoholism.

As an egocentric alcoholic I could easily begin to take credit for any success I might have, but that wouldn't really be accurate. It has continued to be true that gratitude for this Power I've found and built a relationship with is essential to my success professionally, spiritually and emotionally.

To be grateful is more than a feeling. It is an action (a practice) - like love is an action. To love someone is to perform loving acts toward or for someone. To be grateful for something is to care for that thing in a way that is representative of my gratitude for it. If I'm grateful for my relationships I nurture them. If I'm grateful for the work I have, I do the work well and take care of my clients. If I'm grateful for my car I take care of it, keep it clean and maintained. If I'm grateful for my sobriety I take action on a daily basis to care for and maintain that. If I'm grateful for a spiritual connection I take action to nurture and grow that connection.

When I keep all of this in mind and take it into the world with me, I tend to stay right sized. I am reminded that I am not the reason I am who I am today, or have the things I have today, or have the relationships I have today, or have some degree of emotional balance, peace and serenity today. I have all of this because I am sober, and I have a connection to and a relationship with this Ultimate Mystery I call God.

Gratitude and God go together for me. There is an old saying that some attribute to the Buddha, "Gratitude turns what I have into enough". I don't know if the Buddha said this or not, but I know it is a truth. I have a gratitude for this life and a God that doesn't pardon me from life but does sustain me in all of life's challenges. Somehow, I am enough and have enough today.

## Beginning a Practice of Gratitude

At the end of the first chapter, I talked about beginning to look for gratitude and identifying those things, events, or situations for which we can be grateful. Now, we are going to put this into a practice.

Why? If you're like me (and a lot of us), sometimes you might feel like the experience of life isn't quite living up to what it should or could be. Maybe you can feel a little defeated before you even get out the door in the morning. For any number of reasons, a little encouragement can always be a help. We are going to go beyond a feeling of gratitude into a practice – actions that we can take to shore up a state of well-being of mind and spirit. We're going to begin to take action, regularly, in order to bring about a new, changed attitude and/or mood.

**First**, you might begin by looking back at your list from chapter one. Or you can begin a new list now. What is something you can be grateful for right now? – a relationship, your job, a friendship, your sobriety if you're in recovery, …anything you want to list.

**Second**, having identified gratitude, what can you do today to take care of that thing for which you are grateful? How might you maintain, strengthen, or nurture it? What can you do to express your gratitude for it?

*Example*: *I'm grateful for my significant other. So, I am going to go out of my way to make sure they know it. I am going to ask them how they're doing and just listen. I'm going to let them know I love them.*

*Example*: *I'm grateful for my job today. So, I'm going to go to work and look for ways to be of service to my coworkers and the people I work for. I'm going to do the very best work I can do today.*

*Example*: *I'm grateful for my home today. So, I'm going to do something extra today to make sure it is clean and well maintained.*

*Example*: *I'm grateful for a spiritual connection today. So, I'm going to take some action to strengthen and nurture that connection today.*

These are just a few examples. You will have more examples that may pertain more to your situation and your life.

Make a practice of doing this every day. Eventually (and it won't take long), these thoughts and actions will become a working part of your mind. Recall the chapter on *Watering the Seeds*, this is more "watering" of the positive the seeds. The more we water and nurture these positive thoughts and practices, the stronger they become and the deeper the roots grow. They can become such a part of the mind that our minds can begin to process the world through them. We can begin to see the world through a lens of gratitude rather than through a lens of defeat, sorrow, fear, or any other of the negative emotions. ***Gratitude transforms.***

## Chapter 7

# 7 - Growing Up in Public

They say an alcoholic stops maturing about the time his or her alcoholism takes over - or when we start to drink alcoholically. I don't know if that is strictly true or not. But I do know I crossed the threshold of recovery as a child in a man's body. That may sound self-deprecating merely for impact but unfortunately it's true.

When I say 'child' of course I mean emotionally. One of the most destructive traits of the alcoholic is this extreme self-centeredness we seem to be plagued by. We want "what we want" and anything other than "what we want" just *isn't the way it's supposed to be.*

This was certainly the case for me, and I set out in life to make the things I wanted to happen, happen. It was my honest belief that the things I wanted were the things I was supposed to have. And God help you if you got in the way.

I'm not sure exactly where I got that idea. I don't remember anyone ever telling me this, but somehow I picked up that this was what I was supposed to do. Set a goal and achieve it. Decide what you want and make it happen. This was success and success was non-negotiable.

Self-centeredness becomes even more extreme when I decide how other people are supposed to do things, how other people are supposed to behave, how others should be living their lives, and when I start trying to manage the world around me.

"Managing the world" is of course impossible and it looks ridiculous written on the page. But when I got sober and began looking at my character traits - how some of them were completely out of balance - I was shown how much of my discontent, resentment and flat-out anger was based on "people not doing what they should be doing" or "things not happening as they should".

I had no shortage of ideas concerning the way things should go and how *you* should be doing them.

The first few months of sobriety can be a real eye opener. I honestly didn't know how self-centered I was (or can still be). If you had asked, I would've told you I wasn't self-centered at all. This is why a sponsor, or trusted advisor, is so important - someone that can take me through the steps of recovery and show me things about myself that I just can't see on my own. Honest and accurate self-appraisal by an alcoholic in early recovery is next to impossible - and is shaky even in later sobriety.

I had a sponsor that began to show me just how emotionally immature I was - in a very nice way of course. I wrote down all of these resentments and angers I had. We went through them one by one, and he was able to show me that I had made some of my own mistakes in nearly every instance.

I remember being so resentful at a former boyfriend. Time after time on my list of resentments there were cases of him not meeting some expectation I had for him. There were the "needs he did not meet". There were things he did that I didn't think should have been done at all. There were what I considered to be simple norms that he completely missed.

My sponsor asked me if I had ever communicated any of this to him. My response: "no, these are things that he should have just done. This is just what people do". And I meant it. So, I was shown for the first time how the expectations I place on other people were really none of my business to place. I had no business going through life deciding how other people should behave. (Unfortunately, this was news to me.) I felt fully justified in being angry, or at least frustrated, when other people didn't behave in a way I expected them to.

Then there are the things, the people, or the outcomes I want - just because I want them. I had little, or limited, concept of other people's feelings in the dynamics of a relationship - whether that relationship be a one-night stand, romantic, friendship, or professional. I felt a need to control how events would turn out and anyone I might be in a relationship with – either actively or passive aggressively (my personal favorite).

In my active alcoholism, I felt that other people should be able to toss their feelings aside just as easily as I tossed those people aside when I was finished with them. If they had hurt feelings, it was their job to get over them. I couldn't have seen how it might have been my job to change. Unfortunately, this is one I had to learn over my first couple of years in sobriety. (Change can take a while.)

This is the growing up part. I had to start owning my own bad behavior and making it right as I went along. I could no longer just hurt someone's feelings, run roughshod through someone's life, or betray someone's trust and walk away guilt-free. That isn't how sobriety works. That isn't how being an adult works.

When I hurt someone, I have to let them know that I know I did that. Then I have to make it right. And then take action to change. I have to do the work to remove that behavior from my life.

Doing all of this in a fellowship of recovery can be a little embarrassing and painful at times. We're honest with each other and we talk about what's going on. We talk about where we are in our process of recovery and the mistakes we make along the way. Then we talk about the solution - always get to the solution.

We sort of become this extended family - which means we end up knowing a lot more about one another than we would like sometimes…possibly a blessing and a curse (but definitely a blessing).

I have done some growing up in public. There is some intrinsic strength in that. We are able to support one another and learn from one another. I've heard so much shared in meetings that I have been able to use in my own circumstances. And when I have shared the wreckage I've caused, along with what I've done to repair it, someone else may have been able to use that in their life.

The temporary embarrassment of making a dumb move in life is far outweighed by the immense feeling of support and love from a group of people that are just like me.

This is really what it's all about. I came into recovery feeling so desperately alone and along the way I found this family of people that just want the best for me. They really went -and still go - out of their way to not just tell me what they do to get better - they show me. We take each other "by the hand" and tell one another that we've done that thing too, we've felt like that . Then we show each other what we did to get through it, so we never have to do that thing or feel that way again. They took me through it so that I could in-turn take someone else through it.

Learning to be less self-centered isn't an overnight task. Trust me, it's still happening. It's a process and it takes time. Gaining some emotional balance has taken some time and it takes practice. Putting other people before me - their wants, needs and desires - never sounded like anything I'd really want to do, but I find myself doing it.

I was forty-four years old when I started growing up in public. I had forty years of unlearning and undoing to do.

So much of what I know about living today I have learned since beginning a process of recovery and getting closer to the Power greater than me that will nudge me in the right direction - if I let it. I have learned how to treat people the way they should be treated. I have learned how to be honest with others and, just as importantly, with myself. I have learned what it means to be trustworthy. I have learned the importance of understanding and compassion. I have learned how to love.

I thought this whole sobriety thing was about not drinking. Not drinking was just the start. I had to stop drinking so I could learn why I drank in the first place. And then I had to learn to live in a way that would keep me free from needing a drink and then free from even wanting one. I found all of that while growing up in public.

The trick is sticking to the path - this journey. It can be so easy to just let up a little bit; maybe take a break for a little while; or, one day just decide that I've grown enough for now. Letting up or taking a break just aren't options for me. Having lived this life for a while now, I'm not sure I would take them if they were. I really like this life I've found. I enjoy being on a spiritual path. I like waking up in the morning to spend some quiet time with the Power that keeps me sober and allows me to find the peace available in every moment. I treasure the time I get to spend with someone else that just needs to talk and that might want to pick up the same tools that have been given to me.

Growing up in public might sound like a bad gig at first. But the incredible life I get as a result makes every growing pain worth the effort. I get to keep moving forward…keep rowing the boat.

## A Reflection - How Are We Showing Up?

Here is where the rubber really begins to meet the road, so to speak. To begin looking at how we show up in the world - on a regular basis – can be eye-opening to say the least.

How do we show up in our relationships?

Are we taking most of the time? Are we expecting something from others a lot of the time?

How dependent are we on the actions of others to find peace, worth, or satisfaction for ourselves?

Are we looking for what we can get out of the world, a situation, a person, an event - or - are we more interested in what we can contribute, without expectation of reciprocation?

My answers to the questions above began to shed light on my own ability to move through life with some degree of grace and maturity. It is very difficult for me, and I believe for any of us, to begin to make progress without first beginning to get a clear understanding of how we're showing up in the world... *"just how self-centered am I?"*.

Just to be clear, receiving something or having some expectation isn't bad or negative in and of itself. But when my reactions to unmet expectations throw the balance off in my own life, they can begin to negatively affect my ability to find happiness and live a contented life. And when my motives for receiving, or expecting to receive, are unbalanced and self-centered, I run a much greater risk of being dissatisfied, experiencing a hurt ego (hurt feelings), and responding out of a fear-based emotion (anger, frustration, jealousy, worry, irritation, annoyance, cheated, etc.). This is a near universal truth. I am not nor have I met anyone immune to this truth.

Once I begin to see the nature of some of my difficulties, I can begin to deal with them more effectively and begin to watch for them as they creep in. If I don't like what I see, I can take action to change. I can't go through life expecting the world to change around me. When I change, my experience in this world changes.

Diligent self-examination and the ability to attain an accurate self-appraisal, are crucial to any process of improvement. If I don't have an understanding of the source or genesis of my discontent or dissatisfaction in life or with my circumstances, I will likely remain lost on my own rudderless boat. I can't know how to get where I want to go unless I know from where I'm coming.

# Chapter 8

## 8 - Row the Boat

I heard an Austrian monk once say that the spiritual journey was like being on a rowboat and *we* have to do the rowing…and probably stop along the way to fix a leak here and there. Then he said this: *the real difficulty comes when we realize that all the rowing we've been doing is just work we give ourselves to keep ourselves busy "doing things" rather than seeing we're already there - and the thing between us and a greater spiritual connectedness is actually "us".*

One of the first notes I made to myself in the first year or so of a steady contemplative (meditation) practice was the realization that the thing, or things, that were between me and God were things I put there. We learn in the earliest work of getting sober that things like resentment, anger, fear etc. can hinder a relationship with God. But this was something different, something more.

I realized that what I thought about God could come between me and God. The things I thought God would or wouldn't do, could or couldn't do, or even what I thought God was or wasn't - these things were blocking me from a growing experience with God. I talked about this a little bit in the chapter *God of our Understanding.*

It's very difficult for the brain not to add attributes to an object in our mind. We're going to do it. So, I have to make sure I leave my mind as open as I can. I have left room for my description of this Mystery that I don't really understand to change over the years. This decision to maintain a level of open mindedness is a conscious decision and it takes a conscious, continual effort to maintain it. As my relationship with God has grown, how I think about God has changed.

I've had many great teachers - both living and dead. Not surprisingly though, my world hasn't been flooded with people interested in pursuing a contemplative lifestyle - or at least a life somewhat shaped by a consistent meditative or contemplative practice. Luckily, there is a near endless supply of video and audio recorded lectures, talks, and interviews, as well as the written word concerning these practices. We seem to find our fellow travelers once we begin the journey.

Which brings me back to "rowing the boat". I was going to have to build the boat, make the oars and then find the river. And now, looking back, I wouldn't have it any other way.

I found so many resources to support my journey. I found authors like Thomas Merton, Richard Rohr (who has done quite a bit of work related to recovery), The Cloud of Unknowing, and so many more. I also found the classic mystics: Meister Eckhart, John of the Cross, Teresa of Avila, Julian of Norwich and the list goes on.

I began studying and learning with a voracious appetite.

I found Thich Nhat Hanh - and I fell in love again. Here was an incredible man who devoted his life to helping other people – in the East and the West - find a way to lead and live peaceful, contented lives. He talked about the Buddha *and* God. He talked about the Buddha *and* Jesus. And he helped me see that the Western ways and the Eastern ways weren't so far apart.

One thing I was pretty sure of…after the life I had been living, I really wanted to find an easier way to live this life. I had already felt some peace and serenity and I really wanted to hang on to it, to whatever degree possible.

I began building this little boat of loosely woven understanding, faith, a lot of hope, and a practice of meditation that seemed to be working. And I had two oars - one Eastern and one Western. This has been an incredible kit at my disposal.

In the chapter *Watering the Seeds* I touched a little on the idea of a diligent, persistent practice, but that was just a beginning. I've been rowing this boat for quite a few years now. And the experience has been nothing short of incredible but above all - nourishing.

In only a few months I'd established a daily practice. I genuinely started enjoying this time in the morning. I enjoyed it so much in the morning I'd do it again in the evening or at night. I started to feel different. I began to respond to people and situations differently in my daily life - not all the time, but it was a beginning. For alcoholics in recovery, this whole process of meditation goes beyond relaxation techniques or stress reduction. We must learn to think differently. We must learn to act and react differently. Remember, I said earlier that left untreated we are self-centered to the extreme.

We meditate with the expressed purpose of slowing down our reactions and improving our ability to "hear" or connect with that little voice in us all that will tell us the right thing to do. We call this *Conscious Contact with God* - that little voice in us all that will nudge us toward the right way if we will pay attention to it and surrender to it.

The longer I practiced, and the more regularly I practiced, the more easily I could get to that little intuitive voice inside. I started behaving differently. Suddenly I realized I was interested in being of service to other people. I started taking service commitments - and enjoying them. I started looking outwardly more. I started looking for ways to be helpful.  Some of this was out of pure gratitude for not having to live the way I had been living before, but I can now see that most of it was a result of being changed from the inside out.

By the time I hit my third year of sobriety I was in full stride. I remember sitting down with my sponsor at the time and having a discussion about what it means to *keep* living sober. After the first year or two life tends to even out. Employment is likely under control. Finances are at least in better shape - without as much concern for day-to-day survival. Most of the "big stuff" is taken care of. Then I would have to keep going.

I found out I was right on course. There comes a time (usually around years two or three of sobriety) when we begin setting up a life. We begin to look a little more clearly at the path ahead and begin to learn how to just live a sober life – physically and emotionally. That may sound anticlimactic to a non-alcoholic or a non-addict, but to one of us it is a dream. We take what has gotten us sober up to that point and continue to use these spiritual tools as a way of living.

Years three through five were all about beginning to live my life on spiritual principles. And it was a beginning. For this alcoholic that meant pray, meditate, go to meetings, read, study, help others, work and take the next small action indicated in front of me - as a way of life. This was to be my recipe for a successful, peaceful and contented life.

This is rowing the boat.

There have been years with small incremental growth - nearly imperceptible to me. And then there have been jolts forward (usually following some sort of emotional pain). I have to row through the calm clear wide-open waters and through the rapids too.

I was fairly content for those years to just keep doing what I had been doing. I'd have my little quiet time in the morning. I'd go to meetings. Life was just fine. No big "ups" and no big "downs". Everything was just fine.

Then 2020 hit. In March 2020, Dallas (the city I live in) shut down. The COVID-19 Pandemic was in full-swing, and none of us knew what was happening or what was going to happen.

Our meetings shut down. We started having some meetings on Zoom but for some of us that format somehow made conditions seem even worse. We couldn't meet in restaurants or coffee shops because there weren't any. In the very beginning we couldn't even meet in outdoor settings like city parks or open lawns.

I can barely put into words how grateful I was, and still am, that I had established a consistent practice of spending quiet time with God during the years leading up to the pandemic. I know this practice gave me exactly what I needed to get through that time with a sense of well-being I'm sure I wouldn't have had otherwise.

My workload slowed down considerably through 2020 and early 2021 but didn't dry up thankfully. As a result, I was granted the incredible gift of time. I had the freedom to devote so much time to a more in-depth study of Buddhism and early Christian mysticism. I dove into Dharma talks by Thich Nhat Hanh and read everything I could get my hands on. I started reading the great mystics like Meister Eckhart, John of the Cross and Teresa of Avila. And I was able to practice. My meditation practice grew. When my practice grew my experience grew as well.

To continue (or belabor) the metaphor, my oars were able to hit deeper water. If there is a silver lining for that period, this would be one for me at least.

The pandemic forced me, willingly, to go deeper. I felt I needed a deeper and more fulfilling relationship with God. And that's exactly what the practice of Centering Prayer is - it is a relationship with God. The method of Centering Prayer as I practice it practically mirrors a Chan Buddhist method of meditation known as 'Silent Illumination'. I love how the Eastern and Western practices can dovetail so well together. With little else going on, I was able to spend a solid year intensely focused on growing my practice...another great a gift.

I think the pandemic changed just about everyone and everything. It's been four years now, as I write this, and nothing is quite the same - I'm certainly not. Since then, I have continued my study and my practice. I did let up for a few months when the world seemed to be coming back to some sort of normal. I'm human. But when I backed off my spiritual exercise, I seemed to get spiritually weaker. Once I noticed it, I didn't like the feeling. Life keeps steering me back to this work.

In early 2023 I had a return of depression. I have had a history of major depressive disorder. This was a big one. Looking back, I can see where it started coming on, but I couldn't see it at the time. I started getting quieter. I started spending more time alone. I wasn't going to eat with people after meetings. I'd rush straight home. And then one day there was a major shift. There was a darkness and an aloneness that came over me that I could not shake. I could barely get up. Needing to get ready to go somewhere, I would go stand in the closet for ten or fifteen minutes unable to pick anything out to put on.

I knew I felt horrible, but it was a feeling I couldn't do anything about. And when it got that bad, I just gave in to it. It was too heavy to move.

Life felt bearable for moments though when I would meditate - during my periods of quiet time spent with God. This is when consistent, persistent practice paid off again. I still had my time of Centering Prayer every morning. It was the only time I felt "light enough" to exist.

I used it as a form of healthy escape – a respite. I just kept doing it. It was the only thing I knew to do. I would spend thirty minutes in quiet contemplation when I woke up and again two, three, four or more times throughout the day. It got scary there for a few days, but in quiet contemplation I could hear that little voice inside. Just like in early sobriety, when life felt too heavy to carry, I knew to just keep putting one foot in front of the other.

I finally had a breakthrough in a morning meditation. I knew what to do and had the strength to do it. I called my doctor and I talked to my sponsor (I had been talking to my sponsor throughout this time anyway). I told my doctor what was going on and he said, "ok, we need to get you leveled out". Within a few days I was back under a doctor's care for my depressive disorder.

Meditation, contemplation, nor any of the other practices I write about in this book are cures for or answers to any medical or psychiatric maladies. If you are suffering from or feel like you're suffering from a clinical depression, seek professional help. The practices I engage in help bring me to the Truth. The truth for me was that in the case of my clinical depression I needed, and continue to need, a medical solution for a medical problem.

These spiritual tools are solutions for spiritual problems. There is no pill or medicine to make me less self-centered, to cure alcoholism, or to make me a more spiritually centered, pleasant, contented, happy human being. That takes work.

That event was so incredibly painful. I've tried to describe what has happened since then so many times and in so many ways. I fall desperately short every time. I was able to be so broken - I say I was "cracked open". I was left raw - emotionally and spiritually exposed.

In the days and weeks recovering from that depression, I noticed I wasn't seeing anything or anyone quite the same anymore. So much of what I'd read and studied made sense to me on a completely new level. I knew what Eckhart meant when he talked about seeing with the eye of God – "my eye and God's eye are one eye". I had experienced brief - very brief - moments of communion. I knew what it meant that God was there, had always been there and would never leave.

I suddenly knew what John of the Cross meant when he said that to go to God we must "go a way that has no way". We must go by faith which is beyond understanding and experience. And when Teresa of Avila wrote of meeting God through our imperfections - not our perfections.

I was permitted to find the part of me that is always with God and where God is always with me – at the center, or the ground, of my being. I was able to commune with God in my brokenness. I felt I had finally discovered and touched upon that divine spark in me that is indestructible.

*I know now that I am stronger than I've ever been where God
and I came together in the cracks of my brokenness to mend.*

I don't know why it takes such an earth-shattering event to
bring about a change like this. Maybe it doesn't have to, but it seems
to have happened this way for me. I'm sure there isn't any science to
back this up but maybe the bigger the pain the more opportunity we
have for change on the other side of it.

I do know this though, I am grateful. I'm 99.99% sure I
wouldn't have the spiritual connection I have today without the pain
I've experienced.

That old saying is *somewhat* true, "pain is inevitable, suffering is
optional". I don't know that all suffering is optional, but I do know it
can be temporary. I'm grateful for a practice today that makes
suffering temporary and for a practice that makes use of the pain. I'm
grateful for a practice that tacks growth onto the pain and suffering
that I have been through; and for a practice that allows even
incremental growth when life is smooth sailing.

All of this takes me back to the opening of this chapter. I have
kept myself busy rowing, taking breaks along the way, fixing a few
leaks here and there until I suddenly realized that I'd been there all
along. The journey isn't over a distance. Realization comes in an
instant. The instant I turn, or open the door, or glance to see - I can
change. Gratefully, there are always deeper layers of realization as I
continue to attempt to grow.

*I just have to keep rowing - no matter what.*

# A Reflection on Perseverance

There's one guarantee that comes with 'giving up' or 'quitting': the thing I'm working for, or moving toward, won't happen. If I give up on my program of recovery, I'm not going to have recovery. If I give up on my spiritual connection, I'm not going to have one. If I stop trying to get better, I'm not going to get better. And, if I stop taking action to improve, I'm not going to improve.

I have to begin a process and then I have to continue a process. News flash…continuing is the most difficult part. I don't know if it's human nature or just alcoholic/addict nature, but I know it can be easy to let up on a process of improvement after trying it out for a little while. How many of us have started a better nutrition plan and then stopped it a short time later? How many of us have joined a gym in January only to stop going around late February or March.

The first thing to do in establishing a new practice is to find a community. In Buddhism, we call this a sangha. In other pursuits, it might just be a group or a fellowship. If I'm not sure I'm going to hold myself accountable, it's perfectly reasonable to find someone or a group that can share accountability with me. In recovery we have groups that meet regularly, and we share our paths, our experiences, and our strength with one another.

Perseverance requires an element of discipline. I've never had much discipline. It has been a learned skill. But it can be learned.

Unfortunately, there isn't a magic pill to take or a wand to wave to suddenly provide the perseverance required to make change happen. It just takes consistent, continued effort. Once I started to get the full effects of living life this way, I couldn't get enough – I can't get enough.

*Perseverance eventually becomes a part of character rather than a discipline induced chore.*

## Chapter 9

# 9 - No Matter What

"No matter what!" "Don't give up, *no matter what.*" "I know I have to stay connected to God, *no matter what.*" "Suit up and show up, *no matter what.*" These are phrases (or phrases similar) we use and hear quite a bit in the rooms of recovery.

Persistence is central to staying sober and attempting to grow emotionally and spiritually. *Giving up* is easy. *Letting up* is easy. *Continuing* can be difficult. But this is the challenge we have. I've never met anyone that didn't have some degree of "ebb and flow" in the intensity with which they "persist". No one can be dialed up to "10" every hour of every day - it just isn't possible.

There is a great line in the program of recovery I am a member of: "Do not be discouraged". We hear it at the beginning of every meeting. But it can be easily forgotten or overlooked. This, in my opinion, is one of the most important lines we have. It can be just as easy to get down on ourselves as it is to forget that very important line.

The "no matter what" isn't meant to imply any sort of perfection. It is meant to imply that we *are not* perfect. Life is not perfect. So, when we do mess up or when we are faced with some seemingly insurmountable obstacle - that's the "what" in "no matter what".

"I really screwed up when I argued with my coworker today. But I'm going to suit up and show up tomorrow to make things right with him - no matter what."

"My partner and I finally came to the realization that our relationship is over. We're splitting up, but I'm going to stay spiritually centered today - no matter what."

All sorts of things in life can be painful, disappointing, or heartbreaking. But none of these things have to take me away from or hinder the relationship I have with my Higher Power. I can meet even the most discouraging and painful moments of life with a determination and an inner strength granted me as a result my spiritual connection.

### Listen - no matter what.

I knew a lovely lady in early sobriety who battled some debilitating psychiatric health issues. There were many times she would struggle to communicate what she wanted to say.

I'll never forget (I hope) when one day, about eight or so years ago, she shared with me something I had to write down. She said, "Every conversation I have with my sponsor, every conversation I have with another alcoholic, every meeting I go to is a brick in the wall of my recovery. And the more bricks I can put in my wall, the stronger my recovery will be." I've kept what she said close to me since that day. This was her comment on diligence and determination.

I never know from whom or from where some "nugget of wisdom" is going to come. It's easy to judge and to pre-judge. I use this example very often to remind myself that God can speak to me through anyone and through any circumstance – and very often when I least expect it. My job is to pay attention and to listen. My job is to do the work.

### Suit up and show up - no matter what.

Sometimes "suiting up and showing up" can be one of the most difficult things to do. We were about four months into the pandemic in 2020 - alcoholics and addicts were relapsing daily. There had already been a couple of people that I knew of who had committed suicide. I found myself looking around, waiting and wondering why no one was doing anything. People were literally dying without our recovery meetings.

I woke up one morning in July 2020, had my morning meditation and was struck by this statement that used to hang on the wall at a clubhouse I used to go to. We call it our *Responsibility Statement*. I could see it, in my mind's eye, hanging there on the wall. It basically says that it's my responsibility (meaning the responsibility of each individual alcoholic or addict in recovery) to make sure the message of recovery is always available - that when someone needs us, *we* are there.

Now, this isn't me saying "Look at me. I did some great thing." I am 100% perfectly clear that my actions following that morning were not of my own doing but were just me doing my best to *suit up and show up* as I believed God was directing me. I really didn't even know what I was doing or how to do it, but I knew there had to be some kind of a meeting somewhere for us to come together. So, in the middle of a global pandemic I invited a few alcoholics with long-term sobriety, and some that I knew were struggling, to meet in my living room.

Within a month that group had doubled in size. My living room wouldn't work anymore so I found a church that would help us. The church gave us their large auditorium where we could be socially distanced, masked up and temperature checked. All the church asked for was whatever we might collect in a meeting – knowing that wouldn't cover the cost of opening their doors to us.

Word spread - quickly. Our first meeting in that space had 62 people in attendance. This was pre-vaccine and still at the height of the pandemic, but the members of our community needed some place to meet. It grew from there. Then other groups started reaching out to see if they could meet there too. I went to the church, and they opened up their building. We had eight independent groups meeting there within a couple of months.

Anyone could have done this, but someone needed to. The group that started in my living room and then in that church auditorium has the Responsibility Statement in their opening script now - not on the wall. I learned something incredibly important during that time and since. My responsibility is to just show up and do the work that is in front of me and to not let fear get in the way. I very, very often won't know what the outcome will be and sometimes won't even know what I'm doing at all. That's fine. The outcome isn't any of my business. I do the work and how it all turns out is up to this Great Mystery I call God.

There are so may "no matter whats" I could put here. The point is, there is a degree of diligence, determination and work that goes into any amount of sustained transformation. Coming into recovery, I needed to be changed from the inside out. My thinking, my decision-making, my actions and reactions all needed an overhaul.

When I began this journey, I needed to establish a practice of just doing the work whether I wanted to or not - and whether there was some fear attached to the work or not. I needed to establish a practice of picking up the spiritual tools that were given to me - consistently.

This need has not changed. I continue to practice. By not giving up, no matter what, I have been afforded incredible opportunities to see the truth of who I am and the truth of the person I might become.

# A Reflection of Kindness

If you're reading this, you have some resilience in you. You've made it to the middle of this book. There is some determination in that.

It can be a little too easy to begin to focus on the negative aspects of our thinking , character or behavior when we begin a process of improvement. We need to also have a practice of remembering we have some goodness in us and some positive aspects of our character.

In this Reflection, we're going to focus on kindness, compassion and diligence. This is a great thing to do before bed or maybe in the evening after work or after dinner.

Find a quiet place where you can sit with your eyes closed for a few moments.

Call to mind your day. Think about your morning, your drive to work, getting the kids ready for school, your first meeting of the day or that first customer of the day. Think about your afternoon and the interactions you had – conversations, passing on the sidewalk or in the hallway, other drivers on the road, all of the little moments when your path crossed that of another.

Now, call to mind any kindness you showed someone else – a smile given, a pleasant greeting, a concern shown, time spent listening to someone else, a door held open, right of way given…there are dozens of these little moments that we might never think of again, but that might have changed someone else's outlook entirely.

Think about a time when you might have been frustrated with a task but did it anyway. Maybe there was a moment when temper was nearly lost but you thought better of it and walked through it.

Write these down as they come to you.

We often make so many lists of things to do. We've made lists in our previous practices of things to look out for and perhaps some things in us that we might like to change. I believe it is very short-sighted to only name the negative.

We need to remember to reflect on the nice things that happen and on the things we've done well. When I do this, I am encouraged to watch for opportunities to repeat this behavior and I get to feel the achievement of practicing kindness, compassion and diligence more regularly.

Chapter 10

---

## 10 - What Does God See In Me?

Can I join God in seeing me the way God sees me? Seems like a tall order, but what if I could? And what would that even mean?

It is shockingly easy to have a poor or inaccurate self-image. I have found that most people coming into recovery do. And I have found that many of us are faced with, and must continually deal with, these self-image issues as life goes on.

One of the first, and most impactful, things I believe I learned in early sobriety was that *I am inherently a good person.*

I didn't come out of the womb with an expressed intent of becoming a self-centered alcoholic – or a self-centered "anything". I have been afforded the opportunity to learn, on this path, that I am not my actions - my actions are the things I do. I am not my thoughts - my thoughts are what happens in my mind. Anything that I can change - I am not.

Who I am and what I am is a person loved by God – the love of God poured out into every moment of my being. I have all the love of God at my core. That is *who and what* I am.

Now for the bad news. I can get in my own way. My responsibility is to take responsibility for what I do and the thoughts *I engage in*. For this chapter, I'll be focusing on the thoughts I engage in as those precede and prompt the actions I take.

In the practice of Centering Prayer, we have a defined method of not engaging in thoughts during the time of meditation. Thoughts will come up. That is what the mind does – it produces thought. But during this quiet time with God, I choose to let the thoughts go and not to engage in them.

As a mechanism for letting go, we choose a little word to use and introduce this word as a re-expression our intent to be with God and to let God work within us. Then we turn our attention (in the slightest way possible) back to being in the Presence. The thoughts happen. The goal is just to not engage in them.

So, what does this have to do with seeing myself the way God sees me?

What happens in my mind is the problem. My thinking is the problem. I have gone through life - and still catch myself - attaching myself to my thoughts. The *letting go* of my thoughts in conjunction with the *turning to* God is the mechanism through which I can begin to let my old ideas go so they might be replaced with a clearer more accurate understanding.

Most of us have a habit of believing what we think. If I think it, it must be true. Right? What I know is the truth. Right?

Maybe, maybe not.

There is a lot of misinformed thought in my head - things I've imagined other people thought about me, things I've heard people say about me, things I've read about me, and the things my own self-loathing self has told me about me.

Guess how much of the above has been about me being the love of God itself?

Correct - none.

I had to begin very early in this journey (without knowing yet that this is what I was doing) to train myself not to identify as my thoughts. It started by listening to someone other than myself: my sponsor, friends in recovery, people in meetings. Early in recovery we do an exercise referred to as a Fear Inventory. I discovered fears I never knew I had. I discovered fears I didn't even know were fears.

*I discovered my fears can cloud my ability to see me as God sees me.*

I found out that my jealousies were actually fears. When I judge people, that's based in fear. When I judge myself, it's based in fear - fears that I won't or can't measure up, fear of not being good enough or a fear of being less than the people around me. My ego loves fear. My bloated ego uses fear to create separation between me and those people I perceive to be "better than me".

By bringing this practice of letting go from my time spent in meditation into my daily life, I can begin to let go of these thoughts that creep in when I'm out in the world. When I am driving down the street, or interacting with coworkers, or dealing with whatever life has in store for me that day, I can *let go* and *turn*.

Over time, rather than identifying as my thoughts I can become the observer of my thoughts. I *can* begin to sort through my thoughts and choose the ones to engage in: "this one is self-loathing", "this one is self-centered and self-serving", "this one is loving, caring and God-centered", etc.

It has taken some time, but the vast majority of the fears that were on that list - and there were quite a few - have been worked through. (And when they sneak back in, they can be more quickly identified and dealt with.) They can seem so real. It felt like they were all true.

I honestly can't - and don't want to - imagine a life without a practice of prayer and meditation. This practice *is* my relationship with my Higher Power - a Spirit of Universe that seems to bring calm and clarity where, historically, it has been so lacking. This relationship I have developed, and continue to participate in, has given me more clarity on who and what I really am than I can put into words. (It's taking an entire book to try to do so.)

Even when life seems chaotic, I can stop and spend a few quiet moments with the God of my understanding. I can pause for a couple of seconds or for twenty minutes or more to just be in the Presence. This process is an amazing exercise in letting go of all of the chatter in my brain, all of the thoughts and emotions, and all of the images than can inhibit my ability to see clearly. Then I can get enough clarity to see reality as it is - without the noise in my brain coloring or shading it.

Not only do I begin to see life as it really is and others as they really are, but I also begin to see myself as I am. I am faced with the things I've done and the words I've said, but I also see that I am not those things. All that behavior can be changed with the strength and guidance of this Mystery I choose to call God.

I was about a year sober when I finally realized I wasn't this bit of "damaged goods" destined to remain damaged. I had been taking the actions necessary to bring about change in my life and that change had begun to take place.

When I spend the suggested time of silent contemplation in the morning with God, I somehow have this power to take into my daily life with me. I gain enough insight or intuition to begin to make different choices and I don't have to carry those fears around with me.

Over time a confidence has built up inside me that tells me I can be a person useful to other people. I can be of use to myself. It told me I would be able get back into my profession and do good work. I could even show someone else how I had begun to recover from this horrible disease.

I began to perform what I would come to find out were loving acts. It felt good. There I was, this once self-centered, egocentric alcoholic, actually enjoying helping other people. So, I kept doing it.

I keep doing it. This is what brings me the most joy - helping someone else find their way to a relationship with a God of *their understanding*.

When I think about joining God in seeing me the way God sees me, these are the things I think about. I know God sees the real me, the me deep down, the me that can be disguised even to my own eye, with all sorts of shame, remorse or guilt.

When I make the effort to do the things God would have me do, I get to show up as and realize the person I really am. I get to see that I'm not less than anyone else, or destined to failure, or destined to be a drunk, or any of the other painful things I thought about myself. I am simply the love of God in me - unmasked, unadulterated, full-strength love. My job is to stay in contact with that love, to the best of my ability, on a daily basis.

Rather than continuing to spend a lifetime striving to be more than I perceive myself to be, I can expend the effort to let go of the fear-based thinking that prevents me from seeing reality. I have perceived myself to be less than I am because I did not see the divine nature in every living being – myself included. I am not the labels and identifiers I have attached to. I am a person capable of all of the love of God – if I choose to *let go* and *turn to* God.

## A Reflection on Our True Nature

If I might borrow from the Franciscans and St. Francis of Assisi, "all of creation is the reflection of God".

I am, and you are, the goodness and the love of God poured out into every moment of being.

The butterfly, the mosquito, the blue sky and the dark stormy sky, the crystal-clear mountain stream, the mud, and the muck, at our best and at our worst – we are all created by, loved by, and loved into being by God, Nature, the Universe, the Mystery.

We all have the source of strength within us to peer through our fear and see the nature of our true selves – not separate from God.

Sit and contemplate your true nature.

We are the love of God, capable of the love of God, without innate discrimination toward anything or anyone – including ourselves.

In this love, incredible transformation is available and possible.

Smile to yourself and smile to the world around you.

With eyes closed, breathe these thoughts into your mind and into your heart.

## Chapter 11

# 11 - Forgiveness is Freedom

One of the most difficult things I have been faced with is the idea of forgiveness. I had certainly done some things that caused pain in other people - and, I would have to make amends for those things. But what about the things that had been done by others that harmed me? I mentioned earlier that my older brother and I had been physically abused as children. My family tossed me aside when I came out and I haven't had contact with them since.

I had no idea how to forgive people for harms like these. I carried this pain with me for decades and relived it over and over again in my head. To carry around that much anger and that much pain for that long would be detrimental to anyone, but it is especially harmful for an alcoholic. For us, holding on to resentments can quite literally be fatal – it nearly always leads back to drinking or using.

The small stuff was relatively easy to let go of: getting fired, being dumped by a significant other, being treated in some way other than how I thought I should be treated generally, etc. These were all situations where I could see the mistakes I had made that led - at least in part - to the outcomes I disagreed with or was hurt by.

But abuse and getting disowned for existing as the human being I am - how can I just forgive and move on?

I discovered I didn't really know what *forgiveness* meant. I somehow had it in my head that if I forgave someone then I had to be OK with what they did. I thought when I forgave someone, I had to be willing to let them back into my life like nothing had ever happened and then live happily ever after.

Yet another thing I had wrong.

I found out through this process of recovery that I would have to find some way to forgive people if I was going to be happily sober. I learned that forgiveness was just letting go of my need to punish them for what they did or to be able to stop wishing some form of retribution on them - not suddenly excusing it.

The Buddha likened holding onto anger to holding onto a piece of hot coal in your hand. I can hold my anger toward another and hold it and hold it, but the only one experiencing the pain is me. When I hold onto anger, I hurt myself. The anger I keep for someone else has nothing to do with them and everything to do with me, my mental and spiritual well-being, my health, and my ability to be at peace.

I wasn't going to have to invite anyone back into my life. As a matter of fact, in some cases my own well-being would mean staying away from some of those people.

Could I get to a point of letting go of the ill-will I had for the people that had caused me pain as a child? Could I drop the coal? That would take some time and some work.

The first thing I had to realize was that the actions that caused me harm were no longer happening. I was clinging to the pain and reliving the events in my own head. I'm not victim blaming myself here - but for my own mental and emotional health, I do have to get to the point of recognizing that the past is not the present. I'm not talking about pushing trauma down or hiding it away. Trauma needs to be dealt with in settings with professional help as needed. I'm just talking about not having to rethink and rethink and reimagine the events and then what I could've done, or should've done, or what I'd say if I ever had the chance to confront them, etc etc etc.

Like so much of everything in this process of growing a spiritual connection, it's all about beginning and continuing. But I had to start the work. If I don't begin, there will be no process and no recovery.

There is an *exercise of understanding* that was shown to me. That isn't what we call it in the program of recovery I am a member of, but it's what it is. It is a process of looking at the other person as though they might have a spiritual illness just like me. That illness or some other deficiency may make them act in a way that causes harm to others, just as I had done. If I can get to the point of understanding the other person might by ill too, then I might be able to show them the same compassion I would want for myself.

That exercise worked remarkably well for me - most of the time. But there were some people in my family that my pain had kind of dehumanized. I couldn't see the parent as a person anymore. I could only see the harm they had done. Then I was given an incredible gift.

I was told to make a list of all the helpful things a particular parent did for me. It was so hard to start that list. I stared at the paper with a pen in my hand.

Then the first item: *taught me how to cook*.

Then another: *shared a love for music with me*.

Then they started pouring in: *gave me my own room, made whatever dessert I wanted for my birthday* (I didn't like cake), *always made sure I had new clothes for school, taught me how to swim, etc*.

The parent started to become a human again and not the "inflictor of pain". When I began to be able to see them as people again, I was able to begin to get to a place of understanding and compassion. I don't know that any parent really wishes to cause that kind of harm to a child. There was something going on in them they likely had no control over. There was something going in them that made them think tossing a child aside for being gay was the right thing to do.

I don't agree with any of what they did. I don't like any of what they did. And honestly, I don't really like them for what they did. And that's all OK. I don't have to like anyone. I just can't harbor a consistent feeling of ill-will toward anyone - for my own sake. And I can't keep reliving it over and over again.

It is truly remarkable what a little shift in thinking can lead to. I didn't forgive anyone in an instant. But I was able to begin thinking about things differently until one day I didn't hate them anymore. I could honestly say that I was OK.

I still remember everything that happened, but the memory doesn't have authority over me anymore. My memories don't get to dictate how my present is going to feel (for very long anyway). I can grab the tools of understanding and compassion I have been given anytime I want or need them. And I can begin to see others as myself and to see that we're really all the same. I have a set of challenges and you do too.

I spent so much of my life collecting pain that I could use to justify my own bad behavior or my dislike for someone else. Each one of those *pains* or *hurts* collected were bricks put in the walls of my own confinement - they kept me separate with a hovering sense of aloneness.

There is so much freedom in forgiveness. Today, I can take those bricks down just as easily as I put them up - if I'm willing to.

# A Practice for Forgiveness

When I think of the effort it takes to harbor dislike for someone compared to the effort to just let go of those feelings in exchange for a lighter heart, this alone is enough to inspire change. But when I think of the harm my dislike for someone, my anger at someone, or my resentment against someone does *me*, I am reassured of the necessity for a path of forgiveness.

I can water the seed of forgiveness as easily as I can water the seeds of anger or hatred. I can water the seeds of love, compassion and understanding as easily as I can water the seed of resentment.

First, we must choose love over hate, compassion over anger, and understanding over resentment. This is a conscious decision to be made.

*God, grant me the willingness to be loving and understanding and the strength to show compassion.*

Call to mind someone with whom you are angry, resentful, or even someone you hate. If you can't think of anyone, think of someone whom you believe owes *you* an apology or  someone that makes the room uncomfortable for you when they come in. Chances are, there is a reason for that.

As soon you think of them, you will more than likely know exactly why you have this dislike, anger or resentment. Ask yourself if you're ready to let that go. If you aren't ready, ask for the willingness.

If you can ask God, ask God. If you need to just appeal to your own Higher-Good, do that.

*Higher-Good, help me find the willingness to let go of anger, resentment and hatred in exchange for a loving, peaceful heart and mind.*

Remember, you are holding the hot coal in your hand. The resentment you hold is harming you.

Now, begin to focus on one positive attribute that person has. Once you have one, try to find another. Then find one more. It is much easier to find compassion for someone when we see the good in them. See if you can see yourself in them. Have you had similar reactions? Even if the circumstances aren't the same, has there been a situation in which you have been to blame for harm done to another?

When I look deeply into the instances in which I have needed to forgive someone, I have nearly always found some expectation that hadn't been met. Very often, an expectation for someone else to be perfect has been front and center.

"Jane should have done this."

"John shouldn't have said that."

"Cheryl hurt my feelings when she ..."

"My parent should have done better..."

No one on any list of resentments, angers, or dislikes I've ever made has been some sociopathic maniac running from person to person intentionally causing harm. But they have all been people that have had missteps, lapses in judgment, or maybe just thoughtless interactions. I have expected people to act or react in the way or ways I expect someone to act.

Expectations are fantasies we create in our minds for other people to live up to. When our fantasies aren't made real, we can get upset, judgmental, angry or resentful.

Even when I know I'm "right" I still need to let it go. I can be right, or I can be free. Much of the time I can't be both. I choose freedom.

When I look for ways in which we are the same, I water the seeds of understanding.

When I see the other person may have harmed me out of a simple misjudgment or a lapse of judgment, that they may have harmed me out of the sickness of anger or some other soul sickness, I water the seed of compassion.

When I see we are all the same in God's love, I water the seed of love.

I water the seed of forgiveness when I choose to no longer hold someone else responsible for my unmet expectations or for acting out of an illness of spirit; when I choose to show someone else the compassion I would wish for myself, I am closer to freedom for myself.

Remember, forgiveness isn't suddenly liking someone, it isn't deciding what they did was ok, and it isn't inviting anyone back into your life. We're simply letting go of the pain. When I forgive someone, that forgiveness is for me. That relationship may be healed, sure. But for now, I'm deciding to stop harming myself by releasing my grip on the hot coal burning my hand.

# Chapter 12

## 12 - The Illusion of Control

Control - the thing I've always wanted, tricked myself into believing I had, and repeatedly found that I never did.

One of the favorite lines I've heard over the years related to fear and control is: "We're afraid to lose the control we *think* we have over the lives we *think* we're living". I had to sit with this one for a little while.

The idea that I could actually be able to successfully control my own life, or anyone else's, needed to be driven out of me. By the time I reached the doors of recovery, that process had begun as the evidence was piled up against me on this one. I spent my life trying to make the things I wanted to happen - happen. Sometimes things would go my way for a while - often they wouldn't. But even when the thing I made happen happened - it often wouldn't turn out the way I'd pictured it or wanted it to.

The relationship I wrangled went down in flames. The job or the promotion I'd bulldozed my way into didn't turn out to be what I wanted after all. There were times I would find myself in situations that I could try to control for a while but that wouldn't last long either.

Part of this was because I was choosing things, people or situations that were not in my best interest; and part was due to my intrinsic predisposition to dissatisfaction with whatever was.

Not to sound like some kind of sad sack here, everything hasn't been horrible all the time. Sometimes things would work out just fine. But I seemed to find myself focusing on the things that didn't and then trying even harder to "fix it".

Letting go of a compulsive need to "fix it", "change it", or "make it happen" is the challenge. We hear it in our Western culture especially, "MAKE IT HAPPEN!". "You want something? Go after it!" "Don't Give up!" Maybe this is all fine for people that don't deal with any sort of addiction or alcoholism. But I really have my doubts. There are a lot of unhappy people out there.

I know a few "normies" (that's what we call people who aren't addicts or alcoholics) that could really use this lesson. We can get so down on ourselves for not being able to control the universe.

So, when I heard the line I opened this chapter with, I spent some time thinking about it – meditating on it. The last part kept ringing in my head: "The life that I think I'm living". After sitting with it for a while it began to make sense. And it made the idea of "control" even more ludicrous.

There's an "illusion of control" and then there's the *delusion* that I actually know what's going on in my life. The only things I can know are what is happening right now and what has happened in the past. I do not know and cannot know what effects those events are having on my life nor what is going to happen next - the next hour, day, week, month, year etc. When I really got that - I mean really got it - the concept of trying to control anything just went out the window.

I've heard people say the opposite of faith is fear and others say the opposite of faith is doubt. I think the opposite of faith is my need to control. If I have faith that life will happen as it should and that there is a Power out there with a plan for everything (and I'm a part of everything) then why would I try, or need, to control it. Faith is more than a feeling. It's a tool I can use and a reality I can rely upon. Faith is *knowing* and I have to rest in that knowing if I'm going to participate fully in what life has in store for me.

When I look back at my own life, I can see life was going to take me where it was going to take me no matter what I tried to do. All of the things I made happen that weren't for me - they're gone. I am exactly where I'm meant to be despite my best efforts.

I remember very early on this journey - probably thirteen or fourteen years ago - someone told me, "If you're fortunate enough to stay sober, you're going to end up where God wants you. You can go unhappily or happily. The choice is yours." That was his own way of communicating a very Taoist approach - *go with the flow.*

Today, I make an earnest effort to go with the flow. I'm not perfect and catch myself reverting back to "making it happen" on occasion. But that's the point - I catch myself. I usually laugh to myself and smile when I catch it (smiling to yourself is a very nice thing to do); then I can just let it go. The results are near instant.

***When I let go of my attempts to control the universe, I get
instant relief.***

One of the things I treasure most today is the very simple and
easy life I live. Living my life on a more spiritually connected path has
shown me how simple life can be. I always say that I'm out of the
planning business. And I know how crazy that can sound to people.
But I don't really have to make any big plans anymore. I set some
goals like most people, but they're not concrete ,"have to" plans.
They're just some things I'd like if life takes me that way.

It turns out life happens whether I plan it or not. My life unfolds
exactly as it should as I use the skills and talents I have appropriately.
I finish one thing and then do the next thing in front of me.

There's no way in the world I would have planned out a
sequence of events that would take me from driving for a ride sharing
company to being back in my profession and owning half of the firm
I'm now with. Nor would I have hatched a plan that would take me
from scraping loose change together to be able to buy a can of tuna
to being financially secure today. (I always say "today" because…who
knows?)

I don't have to control anything. I really can't control anything.
I have no idea what life I'm living beyond this very moment.

All of the peace I've ever found has been found when I have
stopped fighting, stopped trying to control life and have been fully
present in the present. There is peace and serenity available in every
moment. All I have to do is fall into it.

# A Reflection on "Control"

I can't control my thoughts by force.

I can witness my thoughts and water the positive seeds in my consciousness.

When I water the positive seeds, I move toward a mind of healthier, kinder, more loving thought.

A more loving, caring mind chooses actions that provide a life more beneficial for myself and others.

I cannot control the Universe – not even the little slice I might like to think is "mine".

I can stop resisting what is, accept each moment as it is, and choose my next step with a diligent practice of loving kindness.

When I choose my actions with loving kindness and in agreement with the Universe, I can live a life with much less turmoil and angst.

From a state of acceptance, I can move forward out of love and peace rather than fear and worry.

Freedom is not found in our attempts to control, fix or change. Freedom is found when we cease to resist what is and in each moment graciously accept life as life is.

## Chapter 13

---

## 13 - Living in the Pause

I've struggled a bit to begin this chapter. Not because I haven't known what to say, but rather how to say it. "Living in the Pause" is quite a lofty goal I might reach intermittently at best. But it is my aim - and I believe the aim is more important than the goal.

I've never known a perfect person. I've put people on pedestals only to release them from their perch later - but never a perfect person. To expect that I might reach some level of perfection for myself is clearly a fool's errand. So, why aim if I know I can't actually get there?

Answer: To get better.

But let's back up to what this means - the "pause". What is it?

The pause is simply the space created for a new perspective, a new perception - a space between stimulus and impulse. The pause is an opportunity to witness our thoughts rather than be driven by them. Said another way, it is where and when we can choose to act out of our Higher-Good rather than be controlled by a base impulse.

I'm going to be referring to Centering Prayer and the Chan method of Silent Illumination in this chapter as well. I sort of float back and forth between these two and they sometimes meld together in my practice. Bringing that silence into practice as a method of letting go of thoughts, distractions, mental images, etc. throughout my day, as well as during my quiet time in the morning, has been central in my ability to gain access more easily to the pause in my daily life.

When I first heard of the time commitment…twenty minutes every morning, I was a little discouraged. Twenty minutes seemed like an intimidating amount of time to sit still and to sit silently. But now having practiced for about nine years, that "huge commitment" is no time at all. In fact, when I now consider the benefits, it seems like a very small investment to receive so much in return.

I remember trying to sit still as I first began - when my life was such a wreck. Pretty much all I thought about at that time was how horrible my situation was and how I couldn't possibly think of a way out - or a way back to some kind of what I considered to be "normal". My mind was so busy with "my problems", there was no space in there for anything or anyone else.

What seemed to me like a horrible time to try to sit in silence was actually the very best time for me to begin. All of those tormenting thoughts were what I needed to learn to let go of. It was very difficult to find peace and comfort when my mind was racing with all of the "reasons" I thought I shouldn't be at peace or couldn't have any comfort. How could I when everything was going "wrong"? (Not My Way = Wrong)

Taking twenty minutes every morning to sit in the silence, to invite a Power greater than the power of my self-centered ego into my consciousness, and to just be with that Presence was to be a true game-changer for me.

I found that I could use the 'word of intent' I use during my time of meditation in the morning at time of the day. When distracted by my own thoughts I could use the device of a simple word to effortlessly redirect my attention to the silence and let my thoughts drift by. In the Buddhist method, *Silent Illumination*, a breath is used in the same way as a word of intention – taking a breath as the vehicle to effortlessly express my intention to remain in that presence and not be carried away by my own thoughts.

I was beginning a process of learning to let go of thoughts in my quiet time of meditation every morning so I could bring that practice into my daily life. I was strengthening that "letting go muscle" every morning, through exercise, so that I could access it more easily and more quickly in my exchanges with others throughout the day - or when I found that my own thoughts were getting in my way.

I didn't realize this was even happening until I had been practicing for a few months. I knew I had begun to enjoy that time spent in the morning. I knew it was calming and soothing. I had experienced a peacefulness in the beginning of my day, but I didn't notice any effect on my overall demeanor for some time.

And - let me be clear - this is not an overnight cure for anything. My experience has been a gradual process of learning to slow my reactions down so that my rational, Higher-Good mind can have a chance to make the next decision.

I was about five or six months into the practice of centering every morning before I realized my thought-life had begun to change. I had never had much access to empathy for others. (I was a self-centered alcoholic.) It just hit me one day that I was actually caring for someone else - and not thinking so much about my own problems. I noticed that my reactions to stimuli were different too. Situations that at one time would have angered me were getting a different response - because I was noticing them and choosing a different response. I was able to stop and see that maybe what was needed was some understanding or a little compassion.

Now, this wasn't my response 100% of the time, probably not even 50% of the time, but it was happening. It was a beginning. As I've said before, every task in sobriety or spiritual growth and every beneficial practice in life is about beginning and continuing.

Once I noticed what was happening, I was hooked. I really began to feel and experience a closeness that I'd never had before. I wouldn't have been able to - and possibly still can't - tell you what I was feeling close to, but it was definitely a Goodness that I hadn't experienced before. Some say God, or Creator, or the Universe, or maybe Nature - whatever word works. That's what it was and is.

I now know that I have access to this ability to slow down and choose my reactions - to choose how I'm going to feel about something. My first emotional reaction is going to be whatever it is, but I'm not ruled by that emotion. I get to witness my emotions and examine them. I've spent so much of my life being ruled by my emotions - and not even knowing it.

Living in the Pause is about bringing the silence of contemplation into our daily lives. It is about training our minds to be less impulsive and creating enough space to be the witness to our thoughts rather than being led by or identified by them - and then remaining in that space. The line "we are not our thoughts" is very true but seems so out of reach without a consistent effort or practicing "letting go".

The word "living" implies that this practice should go on for quite some time - perhaps a lifetime. It's important to remember that this is a long-term practice and not a short-term "fix". And the long-term nature is a great benefit. I don't have to get anything right or perfect anything on any artificial timeline. I get to begin and let it be exactly what it is - and get better over time. This is a marathon not a sprint.

The only part that I have to get correct is the "doing". I just have to do it – to begin. This is where diligence comes in. In the beginning it can seem like a chore. But I do a lot of things that are chores. I do the dishes. I wash the laundry. I vacuum and dust. I pay the bills. I do lots of things that aren't necessarily joyful errands for me. You may have other examples that aren't great joys in your life. But we still do them.

The great thing about this "chore" is that it doesn't remain a chore for long. I have found that I actually crave the silence sometimes. I have awakened to a sort of happy anticipation of my quiet time in the morning.

And there are times I feel like just slowing things down midday. My head might get a little "busy", but I can take this break no matter where I am. I can close my eyes for a minute or two and invite the silence into my consciousness. Once I had practiced for a while, I found much more immediate access to this liminal space (the space between thoughts) where I can "take a breath" and set a new course.

What happens when I'm not attempting to live in the pause? I can find myself in a much more reactionary state. Someone says the wrong thing or something didn't turn out the way I thought it should or even worse - I didn't get what I should've gotten (the praise, the recognition, the accolades, etc.) and I'm suddenly caught in this base response mode. I might begin reacting to the world around me without as much regard for the effects on others or how I would choose to if I were acting out of my Higher-Good.

As I go through my day now, I have access to an inner silence. I can stop my day at any time and introduce that little word of intention that has become a part of my subconscious and redirect the source of my thinking. When I feel anxious, angry, judgmental, or hurt, I can introduce my word or simply take a breath with the intent to access the interior silence. Once there, I can be more assured that my reactions are more likely to be influenced by my Higher-Good or a Power greater than me.

One of the most important things to remember is my non-perfection. No one is perfect. So, I'm not going to do many things perfectly - certainly not a lifelong practice. Some have described this as a dance. Sometimes I might have two left feet. There are times I will stumble. But a trip or a stumble won't ruin the dance. I just keep dancing.

# A Practice for Pausing

If you've already chosen a word to use as your 'word of intent', you're one step ahead. If you haven't, you can choose one now or when you begin your morning practice of sitting in the Silence.

As I said in the chapter above, some people use a breath as their vehicle for turning and letting go. But it is important to remember this distinction: we are not simply breathing to calm ourselves (which is a great thing to do). Our word or our breath is used as a vehicle of movement. We are moving from our way of thinking to a new thought. We are moving from being influenced by fear, anxiety, anger, or frustration to being influenced by a thought from our Higher-Good, or God.

This is a practice. So, it takes practice.

It becomes natural after a while. In the beginning you will mostly likely have to set prompts for yourself. If you begin your day this way, it is much easier to remember to pause on your way to work because you were just doing this a few minutes prior. Beginning our day with the Silence sets the tone for our day. And when you forget to pause (and you will, that's what we do), you will realize it much more quickly. You will begin to witness your thoughts and your reactions.

This is a real game changer for so many people. I can't tell you how many future apologies, amends, or just awkward situations I've been able to avoid by simply not saying the thing I would've said or doing the thing that came to mind first.

Perhaps most importantly though, I have been able to access a more peaceful and serene way of being.

1) Begin each morning with a quiet time with God, or the Presence, or the Silence (the titles we use aren't important).

2) Express your intent each morning to gain access to, and maintain access with, your innate sense of this Higher-Good.

3) Bring this intent with you into your day – into the activities and interactions of your day.

4) When you find yourself being drawn into anger, frustration, fear, or anxiety, close your eyes for a moment and bring to mind your word. When I do this, I stop. I bring to mind my word and breathe love and peace into the moment, "peace" followed by a slow, deep breath.

5) Do this a few times if you need or want to. You're creating the space for a new thought to come into. And the space you're creating is one of kindness, compassion and love.

# Chapter 14

## 14 - Thin Places and Meditation

First - What is a thin place? The Celts would say that heaven and earth are only three feet apart but in the 'thin places' the distance is only inches. Plainly, it's a place where you feel like the Presence of God, or Creation, or the Origin of Nature is all around you - and you could almost touch it. People often try to describe an indescribable peace felt there. For some it may be the beach at the water's edge. For others it might be the mountains or a desert. Still others feel it in their place of worship or some historic cathedral or holy land.

What if I could create one for myself - anywhere and anytime I needed or wanted it?

As my experience began to deepen and expand, I began to have a larger hunger. I'd finally begun to realize what my true hunger had always been. I had been starving spiritually and trying to feed that hunger with alcohol and other substances.

As I dove into an exploration of both Western and Eastern practices, I was like a duck to water. I really felt at home in this new pursuit. The first three or so years of sobriety were just about getting and staying sober and learning to live this new way of life. But I began studying in earnest at around my third year. By the time I was five years sober I had very strong Buddhist leanings, but I didn't feel a need to be "pigeonholed" into one religion or one philosophy. I was seeing Truth in so many different approaches to spirituality and religion. The same basic truths were shared by so many.

I've spent the last six years studying Buddhism and early Christian Mysticism intently. These areas of study have guided and greatly enhanced my own spiritual pursuits and most specifically my practices of meditation and contemplation.

I have been using these words 'meditation' and 'contemplation' interchangeably which may seem confusing. In Western context we use the word 'contemplation' to mean what those in the East refer to as 'meditation'.

In the West, the word 'meditation' has usually been applied to a discursive practice - meditating on a certain thought or perhaps a written passage to consider its full or deeper meaning or how it might be applied to one's life or situation. In the Western religious practices, the word meditation is not typically used when referring to a practice of sitting in the silence.

To be clear, when I use the words 'meditation' or 'contemplation' in this book I am speaking of sitting in the Silence.

Many of the early Christian mystics (St. John of the Cross, Teresa of Avila, Meister Eckhart…) would refer to a Prayer of Quiet. My Buddhist journey led me to a very early practice of Chan

Buddhism called *mozhao (pronounced muo jao)* - also called Silent Illumination. Silent Illumination is 'just sitting' or 'just *mind* sitting'.

After some time had passed - after practicing regularly for a few months - I began to get the sensation that I'm really not alone. There is a sense somewhere deep within me of something much more than just me. And if I continue to sit in the Silence, I can get closer to that Source.

This Inner Source is what I sometimes call my Higher-Good - the truest part of me that rests with this Power that I call God at the center of my being. I discovered an inseverable bond between God and me. It has been there all along and is utterly indestructible and unharmable. I would also discover that this bond had been clouded by and layered under a lifetime of learned fears and self-built mechanisms of self-protection. All of those ideas about who I am and who I am supposed to be had gotten in the way of experiencing what and who I really am.

When I started this chapter, I started with a description of Thin Places. If you've been to a place like that, what did you feel there? Did you feel anger, despair, hate, anxiety? Or - did you feel peace, love, or maybe harmony?

This sense of peace, love and harmony is who we really are. When we are so close to the real Reality we can't help but feel who and what we really are. That's why we're drawn there.

A journey into deeper and deeper contemplation creates that same feeling. It starts as a sense of peace and comfort and grows deeper from there. A continued practice takes us further into the center of our being so we can get under all of those layers of junk we've piled on over the years. We can get past the fears of not measuring up. We can begin to experience our truest selves as loving, caring people with an endless supply of that same love from the Source of all love.

I can create my own thin place right in my own living room. I can do the same thing if I'm on a business trip in my hotel room or a city park or anywhere else I want or need to. I can close my eyes, take a few slow breaths and just be. It takes some time and practice, but it works. That saying "a year from now you'll wish you'd started today" is very applicable here.

Now, why would this be important for an alcoholic in recovery - or really anyone needing an overhaul in their thinking? The closer I am to that inner voice that tells me right from wrong, the better off I am. That inner Source isn't just about peace and calm and comfort. It is the voice, or the intuition, that tells me to love rather than hate. It tells me the right thing to do when I'm conflicted. The *still small voice within* can keep me out of a lot of trouble, if I'll let it.

So, the more I practice, the more clarity I get. The more I practice, the more easily I can access that Power within me. It isn't buried so deep anymore - muffled by my own self-seeking desires. It bubbles up to the top much more easily.

Geographic 'thin places' for me are the beach. I can sit there and listen to the waves coming in for hours. I feel completely connected right there. There is a fullness of spirit for me there.

When I sit in the Silence, I can feel the same thing. I feel completely connected. I experience a fullness of Spirit. I gain a closeness to that Power greater than myself that really does seem to fill me with love. I get direction and clarity of my purpose.

All I have to do is sit with the intent to move in that direction and consistently practice letting go of my own thoughts to make space for Something Greater…such a simple task for such an immense reward.

# A Reflection on the Indwelling

I don't know about you, but I never really spent much of my life thinking about thin places, sitting with God, or finding peace and serenity in silence. When I began this journey, it was a new idea for me. I'm grateful that I get to begin this journey again and again with new people I meet along the path.

As I sit to prepare myself to rest in the Silence…in the Presence. I like to bring to mind my oneness with God and God's oneness with me. I am not separate from God. God isn't somewhere else. God is here…my "here" and your "here".

When I feel separate, I have created a separation. Sitting in the Silence is a vehicle for the movement from that separation. To take this one step further, my feeling of separation is an illusion since it is not real.

Shift thought from "inviting God in" to a "lifting of the veil". God is already in. God is at the door, and I simply open it to see the Presence is already here.

Let the idea of God's permanent indwelling settle into your consciousness. Our Higher-Good never turns from us although we may turn ourselves. And when we turn back, we see that God was always there and then we know this Great Mystery will never leave.

There is an indestructible, unharmable part of each of us at our center where we and God come together. Our journey is to that

# Chapter 15

## 15 - The Tyranny of 'Should'

When I realized my ability to find happiness was going to be dependent on my ability to stop placing conditions on it, I found I had quite a bit of work to do. I had fallen into the trap of making my happiness dependent on whether or not things worked out the way I wanted them to - or the way things "*should* go".

I've done this my whole life and I think a lot of us do. I can think back to my earliest memories of school yards and playgrounds and remember looking at the other kids and just "knowing" that I needed to be like them if I wanted them to like me (without anyone telling me I should).

I believe it's one of our most basic needs - to be accepted, to be liked. One of the very first "shoulds" I can recall integrating into my life was: "I should be more like *them*".

Then and there began a lifelong pattern of selecting the people I thought I should be like and doing whatever I needed to do to mold myself in their likeness. "I should act like them." "I should dress like them." "I should like the same things they like and go to the same places they go." "Those are the popular people so what they like must be what people *should* like." Much of the time I do this without ever having the conscious thought that I should adjust my life in the direction they point.

We can see it today all over social media. We even have a name for it, "influencer". It can be so easy to allow ourselves to fall into the trap of letting others define who we *should* be, how we *should* be, what we *should* like, where we *should* go. People are "killing themselves" trying to mold themselves to the image someone else portrays...or wanting to literally kill themselves because they can't.

"I *should* be thinner." "I *should* be more muscular." "I *should* be able to afford to live in this neighborhood or that one." "I *should* have that car." "I *should* be able to vacation more often and in more exotic locales." "I should, I should, I should...I should."

I could list a hundred "shoulds" and then a hundred more.

All of these expectations I place on myself end up being conditions that I place on my own ability to be happy - or content. This, by the way, is how I define 'happiness' - a peaceful contentment. For most of my life I have confused 'happiness' with something like 'exuberant joy' or 'jubilance'.

***Happiness isn't an extreme. Happiness is the contentedness I can feel when I am satisfied with what is as it is.***

There's nothing wrong with seeking joy or jubilance. Who wouldn't want to do that? But these aren't states sustainable for the long-term. What I have found that really introduces a livable peace is the ability to be content in this moment - and this - and this - and this moment.

To find a willingness to be content has been the journey of beginning to *let go* of so many of the 'shoulds' that have reigned over my life.

"Willingness to be content" may seem like a strange phrase. But the willingness must come prior to the actions necessary to bring about contentment – otherwise I likely won't do the work needed to get there. The removal of alcohol and other intoxicants was just a doorway to a beginning for me. I had to be rid of those before I could even begin the work necessary to see the truth behind so much of the unrest in my own mind.

It took some time for the "fog" to clear from my mind after drinking and using for so long. But once I put down the drink, asked for help, and then accepted the help I'd asked for (another significant requirement) – I was able to set out to see just how my own thinking was causing so much of my own trouble. To my surprise, I would learn a great deal of my trouble was directly attributable to my thinking - or "my way of thinking".

'My way of thinking', as it turns out, has been and is my greatest addiction. To keep this addiction in check has taken, and continues to take, consistent effort.

All of these expectations I place on my own life, all the things I believe I *should* be, the achievements I *should* have achieved, begin to shape how I see myself and "who" I *should* be. Thomas Merton would say we often believe we are what we do, so the more we do the more we are. That belief is the mental quicksand that traps so many of us.

I have a habit of believing I'm supposed to be what I think I *should* be, but the more I think I *should* be the less I'm able to realize who I really am - at my center.

My task for today, and every day, is to accept each day, each person, and each situation exactly as they are. I have tried and continue to try to remove the words 'good' and 'bad' from my vocabulary. I don't know what is 'good' nor do I know what is 'bad'. I know comfortable and uncomfortable. I know pain and joy. And I know each of these is impermanent and each is necessary.

The truth is my life is a journey – any life is. I have a loose idea of what I'd like my life to move toward but that's as far as I can go.

I was with some friends one night some time ago and a woman for whom I have a great deal of respect came in and sat down. It was a rainy day and rainy night. She told us about all the plans she'd had for the day and how they were all canceled due to the weather. She then simply said, "I decided to let it rain today". In one simple statement she let go of all of it.

I was thinking about that one day as I looked out my window. I looked at a tree in the yard. I thought to myself "I have as much power to make that tree a flower as I do to get the world to go my way or to make 'him' or 'her' into what I want them to be". I came away from that little bit of quiet time with my own phrase: "let the tree be a tree".

I can't change much of anything in this world other than my own reaction to it. I don't really know how anything *should* go or how or what anyone *should* be – including myself. I don't know how "it all *should* turn out".

My life doesn't have to be reigned by the "tyranny of should". I have a choice today, resulting from a practice of awareness and insight, to look at each situation as it is. I can accept it for what it is - one moment. In the next moment I can choose a reaction. I can choose to smile at each moment and find the contentedness that is mine and reside in a livable peace.

This is freedom. We can find freedom in any moment. Once I knew it was there and available, I could move toward it. When we find ourselves caught up in "our way" or "the way it should be" or "the way it should have gone" or "the way he or she should be" or any of the other traps we set for ourselves, we can stop and ask for the willingness to accept life as it is, the moment as it is, others as they are, and ourselves as we are. We can begin to let go of our demands on life and the expectations we place on it. We can water the seed of acceptance in our mind.

There is a Taoist saying, "by not doing, everything is done". This is another way of saying that when I join in the flow of the Universe, not resisting (or meddling with) it, I can surrender to what is and all will happen as it should.

The Flow of the Universe has never really needed much help from me.

# A Practice – Watering the Seed of Acceptance

How much of your life do you spend comparing your life to someone else's – or – comparing your present circumstances to what they aren't? I know it can be difficult not to. For some reason this is just what most of us do - I certainly have.

When I was sleeping on the floor of someone else's apartment or taking naps in my car in a park because I had nowhere to go (before my car was taken back because I could no longer pay for it) or eating canned tuna because I had $1 to eat that night, it was so easy to say to myself, "this isn't how my life *should* be". It certainly could've gone any number of other ways, but it didn't.

I usually don't get to choose how my life goes. I can try to point it one direction or another, but that's really about it. I don't get to choose how the lives of others go. I don't get to choose how others behave, how they speak, where they go, or if they go.

***Life happens and we respond in whatever way we're prepared to respond.***

'Tyranny of Should' is a phrase I really like – because it is tyranny. All of these "shoulds" begin to rule over us with an oppressive influence on our ability to find peace and happiness.

Take a few moments to think about how much of your own life you compare to others, how you've thought of your situation not quite meeting the ideal you've set for it (financial, romantic, professional, physical appearance, …any life situation), and how any of these supposed shortcomings have impacted how you currently view or have viewed yourself.

Ask yourself how often you find yourself upset at the behavior of someone else…what they said or didn't say, where they went or didn't go, how they showed up or if they showed up at all.

Now ask yourself what would happen if you just accepted each situation exactly as it is.

What if we could just drive the car we drive, be the size we are, live in the place we're living, have the job we have, and so on and so on – and it would all be OK, for today? What if we didn't have all of the expectations on our life and the lives of others?

How much peace could come into your life, today?

For the rest of today, just say that what you have and who you are is enough. Remember the Buddha, gratitude for what we have turns what we have into enough.

When you find yourself comparing yourself to someone else today, stop and say to yourself "I don't have to be anyone other than who I am, today". Remember, who we are is the love of God poured out into each moment. Is there anything more than that?

When I became grateful for a floor to sleep on and grateful for a can of tuna for dinner, what I had became enough. I can live each day grateful for that day and tomorrow I can live tomorrow, free from any tyrannical rule I may attempt to build for myself.

Ask God, or appeal to your Higher-Good, each morning to set you free from the expectations you place on your own life, circumstance, people or situation.

When we do these things, we are watering the seed of acceptance in our mind. When we make this a practice, we allow the seed of acceptance to grow, to strengthen, and to set deeper roots. We begin to view the world through a lens of acceptance. When acceptance becomes a working part of our mind consciousness, we find peace and happiness more quickly and more easily.

Freedom from our own thoughts can be the greatest freedom of all.

# Chapter 16

## 16 - Gifts Hidden in Pain

Emotional pain can be some of the more difficult pain to deal with. For most physical pain, I can take acetaminophen or ibuprofen and know that it's going to go away. Emotional pain has a way of lingering. And when it lingers, it can begin to stir some fear in us.

It doesn't seem like fear, in the way I normally think of fear. But there is this part of me that wonders how long an emotional pain is going to last. It triggers a sense of powerlessness that in itself often comes with fear.

I have learned over these past few years that most often it isn't the event that happened, or is happening, that's causing my pain. It is my resistance to *what is* that causes my pain to linger.

Some emotional pain is a natural part of life. Mourning a death or a loss is perfectly natural, for example. Mourning a relationship that's ending - perfectly reasonable. Being sad or even angry over a lost job seems fine too. But for how long?

It isn't that I shouldn't allow myself to feel the feelings that come with being human. I just need to watch out for staying in those feelings for too long.

One of the more powerful tools I've been given is a process of looking back over my life and assessing the events of my life. How many events did I label as "bad" simply because they were painful at the time? And how many of those events that I labeled "bad" actually ended up being great gifts?

I just have to think back to getting sober after my relapse. I had a partner at the time. We lived together. We both decided to get sober on the same day and about three weeks later we split up. That was very painful and being newly sober I was immediately stricken with loads of fear.

I had no idea at the time that I was getting a gift. I needed to stay sober if I was going to survive. As it turned out he wasn't going to stay sober. Had I stayed in that relationship, it would have been a great deal more difficult for me to maintain sobriety. Imagine trying to stay sober in the same house with a partner who is an active alcoholic.

I labeled that break-up as "bad" because it was painful, and I didn't want it. Those were my two criteria. If it was painful and/or if I didn't want it to happen - it was "bad". I think most of us have the same criteria if we really stop to think about it.

I got fired (deservedly so) from a very well-paying position when I was in active alcoholism. Now, of course I thought this was bad. I got fired. I lost my income. How could getting fired possibly be a good thing? In that moment, of course I labeled it as "bad".

However, getting fired from that job set in motion a terrific chain of events that would lead to me getting sober again. Eventually, not only would my career come back but it would be supercharged compared to the position I held before.

My point is this: I have almost never known the gifts I've gotten *as I have gotten them*. Many of them have come hidden in pain.

Today, I have the awareness that I do not know what lies ahead. If someone hadn't told me to look back on my life and actually take inventory of all of these instances, I wouldn't know now that they were in reality major turning points for me and incredibly beneficial.

I was in a relationship that was ending mid-pandemic, 2020. I had a well-established practice by then and it changed the entire process for me. My partner at the time and I had a simple discussion. We talked and found that our relationship was already over and that we were only realizing what had already taken place. I shared with him that it doesn't have to be more painful than necessary if we don't resist what has already happened. He was in recovery too, so the conversation wasn't too difficult - having the same vocabulary to share.

Of course it was sad. We had shared about four years together. But we could both see our paths were diverging and it was time for new directions for both of us. We accepted what was. It was perhaps the most boring and adult break-up ever. No one acted out of fear. No harsh words were hurled back and forth. This was an incredible gift that I'd received by going through the pain and learning from it before.

Learning to stop when I'm experiencing a painful reaction to some event and *practicing letting go of my resistance to what is* has been incredibly transformative. Today, I can stop and say to myself: "I wonder what the Universe is doing here". I can ask myself: "what gift might come from this"? Then I can wait for the answer.

I don't have to allow emotional pain to linger today and shroud my happiness. I can recognize an emotional pain, care for it, examine why it is there and release it by not attaching to it.

I know I have had many gifts hidden in pain. I know pain does not equal "bad". I can witness what is happening in my life and look for the gifts.

## A Reflection on the Gifts We Have Received

Let's a take few moments to reflect on some of the gifts we've received that may have been hidden in pain.

When I think of a relationship that ended, I like to reflect on what I received from that relationship. Did I receive an opportunity to love someone for a time? What was I able to learn from that relationship and bring with me as my journey continues? What memories can I look back on with a smile?

When I think of the pain felt from a loved one passing on, I like to think of the fun times we had together. I like to think of what I learned of my ability to deal with and experience grief. Am I now prepared to help someone else as they experience a similar grief? What a gift – to be able to help someone else on their passage through grief.

When I think of any loss or unexpected change, I like to look for what life-doors opened as a result. Sometimes space needs to be made in order for the next person, event or stage of life to enter.

***When I look for the gifts, they are there to be found.***

Chapter 17

---

## 17 - My Thoughts or Me

It is amazing to me the power and authority I have given - and can still find myself giving - the memory of something that no longer is or the thought of something that never was.

It can be so easy to become identified with my thoughts and memories. I can begin to think they are what I am: "I am sad." "I am angry." "I am hurt." The truth is, I am none of these things. But I do *experience* them, and my experiences can change. Again, anything I can change – I am not.

I am very grateful today for a spiritual practice that gives me the ability and insight to recognize thoughts as thoughts (memories, thoughts, feelings, emotions etc. are the same in the context of this chapter – the things that happen in my mind). I am not the thought. I am the thinker of the thought. I am not the feeling. I am the feeler of the feeling. I am not the memory. I am the rememberer of the memory. Once I recognize this - and practice it - I can become less vulnerable to the ups and downs I might experience throughout the course of life.

Notice I said, "less vulnerable". I don't know of anyone that has removed all vulnerability, nor do I think anyone should. But I do know people that have trained themselves to be witnesses of their thoughts rather than being ruled by them.

I remember hearing this concept for the first time and not fully grasping the impact of what this teaching could bring. There was the part of my brain that said, "yeah, of course I'm not my thoughts". But when I started looking deeply at my mood and attitude changes, I discovered I was letting my thoughts consume me and I was allowing myself to become them - I was identifying as them. If I felt sad, *I* was sad. If I felt angry, *I* was angry. If I felt lonely, *I* was lonely.

The recognition of this was enough to get some relief. But once I recognized that this was my reality, I wanted to be free from it. Like everything else on this journey, the work required for this additional freedom would require more work - sustained, diligent effort. My Centering Prayer and Mindfulness practices melded in this effort.

As I've said before, every day begins with twenty or more minutes of sitting in the Silence. This is my baseline. I begin every day with an awareness of both nothing and everything at the same time - just sitting quietly with my eyes closed, letting go of any thought, memory or image that comes into my awareness. During this time, I practice non-attachment to the things that are not me.

Then, throughout the day when a feeling arises that my mind attempts to attach to, I can practice mindfulness and look deeply into that feeling. Why do I have it? Is it a rational or irrational reaction? Am I practicing Understanding and Compassion? If not, do these practices correct a view or perspective? Is this feeling rooted in fear or love?

***By looking deeply into any feeling or emotional response, I can begin to see more clearly the nature of my working mind.***

Painful memories can bring up difficult feelings which can often result in self-defeating emotional responses. Earlier in this book I mentioned being physically abused as a child. I identified with those memories for most of my life. And while those memories are real, they are memories. I do not have to let them dictate who I am today. I don't have to let them unduly influence my moods, attitudes, actions and reactions today.

I have sat with all of those memories in therapy, in recovery, and in meditation. Each of these practices has given me insight into the past and what part I play in bringing my past into my present. I was abused as a child. *I am not an abused child today.*

Pain is real. Trauma is real. But having dealt with it, I get to choose, today, how today is going to go. The practices of meditation and contemplation play a huge part in my ability to choose.

If I'm not aware of the thoughts that are influencing my attitudes and behaviors, I am going to have a very difficult time moving toward a different way of being. That move will remain difficult if I don't gain some understanding of how those thoughts affect my decision-making.

Every word I say, everything I do is preceded by a decision. Sometimes those decisions happen so quickly I don't even realize I've made a decision. Slowing this process down is a direct result of contemplation and meditation. In meditation, I can give myself the opportunity to see how my decisions are made and what they are based on. I can begin to see how some painful memories may influence me to make fear-based decisions that could be harmful in some ways to me, or the people close to me.

Not all memories are as traumatic as being abused as a child. What about the more benign memories of a coworker saying something hurtful or that thing the neighbor did a couple of months ago? Memories like these are sometimes more easily missed or dismissed. But my reaction to *that thing they said or did* can very easily taint my interactions with them for months or years to come.

**We can stop and examine our thought-life any time we want to.**

This comes up in my daily interactions perhaps most of all. I was speaking recently with a former friend. Not so many years ago, any interaction with this person would have been greatly influenced by the hurt feelings, the anger or resentment I felt toward him. I remember ignoring him, avoiding him, responding unkindly or dismissively on more than one occasion. He had taken some actions in our past that made a continued relationship untenable. I can now see that in each of the occurrences when I was unkind, I was letting the "memory of something that no longer is" and my feelings based on that memory dictate my current behavior. That dismissive, less-than-kind, resentment-fueled behavior would then directly impact my mood and attitude.

By simply creating the space to examine my thoughts and responses, I could begin to choose a new path – a kinder path. Do I want to have a day influenced by anger and resentment or one based in kindness?

Then there are the memories of the things I did. Shame and regret are two incredibly powerful emotions. I've seen them wreck the lives of people unable to move through them. Learning to feel remorse for things I've done while letting go of shame has been incredibly liberating. However, It is nearly impossible to do so until I've taken steps to attempt to make things right with anyone I may have harmed. But, once I've done all I can to do, I must find a way to move past the shame.

Learning to let go of and practicing non-attachment to my thoughts has been and continues to be a crucial exercise for me. This isn't anything I've been able to do on my own by merely recognizing the need for it. It requires consistent effort. It is a *practice*.

There is serenity and peace available to me in each moment of every day. The obstacles that come between me and peace are the thoughts I cling to and identify with. When I am anxious, disturbed, angry, frustrated – or in any other of a number of negative mental states – I can stop, examine my thoughts, and ask myself why I'm feeling the way I'm feeling. Then I can look deeply into those feelings.

What thoughts am *I clinging to* that are causing *my own* discomfort? What opportunity exists for me to pick up the tools of understanding, empathy, compassion or love? And in picking up these tools, can I begin to *observe* my thoughts rather than *be* my thoughts? Can I begin to observe my thoughts rather than fall prey to them?

***Neither the thoughts I think nor the conditions in which I find myself have the innate power to define me or any intrinsic authority over who or what I am.***

# A Practice for Witnessing Thoughts

Let's begin in silence again.

Sit comfortably, eyes closed, and breathe into the moment.

Let the world around you drift away.

Notice the weight of your body on the chair and feel the floor under your feet.

Feel the air touching your skin. If the air is warm notice it, if it is cool notice it.

Direct your mind toward the silence. Just simply *be* in the Presence.

As your mind continues to work, watch your thoughts float by. Let them move past like clouds passing in the sky. You notice them, but they pass.

If you find yourself fixating on one, turn your attention to the next. In a breath, that cloud floats by making space for the next.

As you inhale, you breathe in a willingness to let it pass. Your exhale carries it away.

We begin to grasp the impermanent nature of thought. How can anything carried away on a breath be who we are? We are the thinker of thought, not the thought itself. Any thought we have about ourselves, about others, about any situation is transient. We begin to understand - our thoughts have no power over us.

# Chapter 18

## 18 - Not the End

I hope you've been able to get something out of what I've put down on the pages of this book. I know I have. I started writing it as an exercise for myself. What has my experience actually been? What do I think about these topics? And, maybe more importantly, what have I learned for myself along the way?

It is very clear to me, today, that everything I have been given, every lesson, any knowledge or experience I have gained is to be shared with someone else. Not every experience will benefit everyone. But some will - maybe even just one. And that's just fine.

I know there have been instances when I've heard a single line from someone with whom I'm acquainted, or someone just passing through, that has impacted me. And I've been able to return to those lines as seeds for growth. I've had the opportunity to plant these seeds in my own life and gain a new experience that can be shared with someone else. That's the source of joy in life for me today.

Any opportunity to share my own experience, some examples of challenges overcome by someone else shared with me, or just some insight I've been granted along my way is what makes my heart sing.

I've been given so much for just trying to get sober, stay sober, and to expand my spiritual life. It seems like a massive treasure for such little effort.

I've been shown the real value of honest living - not just honesty with others, but honesty with myself. I've been shown how to get an honest picture of who and what I am. I can stop, look deeply, and see the honesty of this moment - right here - and find the peace and serenity that resides in every moment.

I've been shown the value of facing my past so that I can be free from it. And I've been shown that by moving through pain I can gain the experience of being "OK no matter what". I no longer feel the need to escape by attempting to take an easy way out.

I've been taught how to forgive and how to be forgiven. And I've been taught how to be grateful for all of it.

I've been given the opportunity to grow up (apparently, it's never too late). And I've learned diligence. I've learned how to fall into Grace and how to give grace.

I've been taught that I am enough in every moment of every day - that God isn't "out there". God is "in here" - in each and every one of us. There's a great saying that says, "no matter where you go, you take your troubles with you". This is true. But there's another great truth I've found, *I take the solution with me too*. The problem and the solution are both within me. I get to decide, today, to which one I will turn.